The ELEVENTH COMMANDMENT

Jimmy O'Connor

1976

SEAGULL

First published in 1976 by Seagull S.A.
P.O. Box 44, St Peter Port, Guernsey, C.I.

ISBN 0 905353 00 5

Printed in Great Britain by A. Wheaton and Co., Exeter

Television Plays by O'Connor

TAP ON THE SHOULDER
THREE CLEAR SUNDAYS
COMING OUT PARTY
PROFILE OF A GENTLEMAN
THIRTY STRETCH
NIGHT OF FEAR
HER MAJESTY'S PLEASURE
ONE OF OUR OWN
WAY OF LIFE
HOME FOR XMAS
THE GENTLE WINKLER
THE TRUMPETER

TALES OF PORTOBELLO, *Short Stories*

For SAINT ANNA MARIA, *my mother, in loving memory*

To my wife, Nemone

and my dear sons, James, Ragnar and Milo

Acknowledgement

To Penelope Eyles, for making me write this book — when I wanted a drink, she gave me milk

Contents

1

A right little tea leaf

It was the 15th August 1971, the Feast of the Assumption and also the Feast of the Madonna of Tinos, an island in the Aegean Sea facing the island of Mykonos where I have lived for over ten years. That morning I called to see Doctor Giovanni to share a glass of whisky. With me was Kosta, another old sufferer who had spent many, many years in jail. He was Greek; I am a Cockney Irishman. We each stood at the side of the doctor as the procession of the Feast of the Madonna of Tinos started.

There are three hundred and sixty churches on this island. The priest, or the pappas as they call him here, carried the crucifix through the tiny whitewashed streets of Mykonos. The whole of Mykonos must have been out on this beautiful morning. As the procession reached Dr Giovanni's balcony he said, "Which one of you is Barabbas? I feel like Jesus Christ."

I said, "It's a toss up between me and him. Let's get back and finish our bottle of whisky."

"No, Jimmy," said Giovanni. "You've had your quota; one glass only."

It was only Easter of 1971 that Giovanni had flown me to King Paul's Hospital in Athens dying from a perforated ulcer.

We went back into his small office. There weren't many patients calling that morning. They were too busy following the pappas through the streets and praying to the Madonna to cure them of their illnesses and sicknesses—no doubt losing my friend Giovanni a few drachmas, but we were happy.

I knew that Kosta had been one of the best pickpockets in Greece. He was now retired and selling souvenirs to tourists; a man full of humour, full of life, full of fun; but also, like myself, suffering from an internal complaint.

Giovanni understood my cockney vernacular better than most Greeks. I used to amuse him. He said, "Jimmy, I like you, but people told me this story about you. I read about you in the newspapers. I read good things about you, but there are gaps in your life. Tell us something about yourself."

I said, "Kosta won't understand what I'm saying and there's nothing worse than someone translating sentence by sentence. He wants to know about me. I also want to know about him. We're never going to, unless I write a book and maybe some Greek scholar translates it."

Kosta went off to sell his souvenirs to blue-rinsed Americans off the tourist boats. He used to take the piss out of them in his own language. They never knew. They were fat, small, tall, ugly and beautiful, a mixture of people. I wondered how many of them were criminals. Some of us are convicted and some unconvicted.

"Come on, Jimmy," said Giovanni. "Tell me about you. Tell me about your childhood."

"All right, Giovanni. Just one more whisky. Plenty of ice, plenty of water. That'll be the last one for the day. We'll go for a walk to the rocks, to Megaliamos, and look towards Delos."

We walked, and took our bathing trunks with us and sat on the rocks. "Where were you born, Jimmy?"

"I was nearly born in the street, George. It was the First World War and my mother was running through Edgware Road during a Zeppelin air raid, trying to make it to Queen Charlotte's Hospital. She just made it. I suppose it would have been appropriate if I had been born in the street. I spent most of my life in the streets as a kid. I was dragged up, not brought up."

My mother was Annie Maria Ball. She married James O'Connor, an Irish seaman, at a church called Homer Row, in Marylebone, just five minutes from Marble Arch. My mother's parents came from Cork. They were dustmen and dustwomen and worked for Paddington Borough Council. My mother was very beautiful, with long red hair down to her waist, and green eyes. She lived in North Wharf Road, Paddington, a slum facing the dust-yard where my grandparents worked.

Granny Ball was a fighter. She wore a cap with a bodkin stuck through the middle on top of her bun. She could fight like a man and would jump off her dustcart, run into the pub, hit my grandfather straight on the chin and throw him out of the pub. She had thick bushy eyebrows, took snuff, pints of mild and bitter, and swore like a trooper. Her husky voice was musical. She had a little terraced house with a small yard at the back; a tin bath hung outside on the white wall and there was a white-washed lavatory with a wooden seat, the usual old pigeon loft, and always plenty of bread and dripping for a ruddy little freckle-faced bastard grandson.

My father's parents, the O'Connors were more affluent, although they also worked for Paddington Borough Council. They had a big house in Paddington in a posh street; no signs of poverty. All the other sons, Daniel, Michael, Thomas and Edward, went to church and served on the altar, symbols of respectability. They were civil servants. Granny's brogue was so strong that you'd get drunk at the sound of it. I never understood a single word she said. I only knew one thing. Every time she opened her handbag it wasn't to give me a penny or sixpence to go to the pictures; it was to take out a small bottle of scotch which she used to swig down.

All the family were very tall handsome-looking Irishmen, and my father was the best-looking of them all. Women loved him, but he was the black sheep of his respectable family. He didn't believe in God, Church or work. He was always drunk and fighting. Everyone was afraid of my father. I never saw one person or relative ever intervene when he used to beat and kick my mother. He cut all her long beautiful hair off with a razor. I remember picking up from the floor the hair that my father had hacked off and putting it in an Oxo tin. I hid it and kept it for months until my mother's hair grew again. Sometimes I used to make a plait out of it and put it on top of her hair. Her hands were scarred from defending herself from razor slashing. She had a scar across her throat where she once attempted suicide. I got used to the bugs, the rain coming through the ceiling, and Irish stew, and my mother's blood spattered all over the wall.

I had two sisters, Kathleen—with blonde hair—and Maria, and a brother, Timothy. We lived in one room and acquired one more after my father had scared the other neighbours out; rent half a quid a week. If you wanted to piss you used a white bucket on the landing; if you wanted to go to the lavatory, there was a communal one in the yard. One night half the ceiling fell down on the bed; I was soaked. I jumped over the bedrail, knocked off the brass knob and cut the top of my cock. I felt silly when the doctor tied a bow round it; embarrassed and humiliated.

My sister Kitty was a very beautiful girl with blue eyes and blonde hair, always singing "Horsey, hold your tail up!" She looked like no one in my family except my own children and grandchildren, but she died when she was about four.

My brother Timothy was a year younger than me, born in 1919. One day we were coming home from the Serpentine. I was a real cadger and used to go into the baker's shop. He used to stand outside. He was very thin-looking. I'd ask for a plate of stale cakes, and I used to nick two or three cakes and slip them under my jacket. I had special poacher's pockets made in my jacket. That particular day he was limping as we walked down Praed Street. He said he had a pain in his back. I took him into the outpatients' department of St Mary's Hospital.

"My brother's got a pain in his leg and I can't get him home. He can't walk properly, he says."

They took him in to see a doctor and then they sent for another doctor.

"Where do you live, sonny?" they asked.

"Paddington."

"Well, take this letter home to your mother and father. Your brother will be staying here for a couple of nights."

I took the letter home and told my mother. She went to the hospital. He never came out again; he stayed in hospital for nine years and died when he was fourteen. He had tuberculosis of the spine, and in those days there was no treatment for it. As he was a Catholic, he was sent to St Vincent's Orthopaedic Hospital at Eastcote, Pinner-on-the-Hill, which is still there. He was put in a plaster cast and was always on a long wheelchair-cum-bed, improvised because anything to do with the Catholic Church had virtually no support from the Government. They were the Sisters of Charity. The ward was like a cowshed. There were no doors; you walked up a wooden slope and there was a line of beds: the children had big heads, short arms or no arms, or were cripples in irons; spastics as we call them today. The Duke of Norfolk's daughter was a sister there. She took my brother to Lourdes eight years running. When they came back one year the headlines in the *Catholic Universe* were 'A miracle took place', and there was a picture of a girl who had never walked before pushing my brother round Victoria Station.

I used to go out to the hospital sometimes on Friday nights. I was just like a piece of furniture out there. They never had proper jars to piss in. I would go round the beds collecting their water jugs, jam jars—pound and half-pound. There was a great big kitchen and I used to go and wash them out and then take them back to the beds. Sometimes I slept there. Firework Night I used to go up there, but every time I went I always used to thieve on my way up. I found two or three easy shops because in those days Pinner-on-the-Hill was in the country for us. I loaded up with chocolates and sweets and various things. A lot of the kids had no visitors at all. Of course, the sisters thought I was a little angel, but when they were having tea in a little canteen of their own, I used to steal a couple of swiss rolls and a few bars of chocolate to take back to the ward.

My brother died virtually a saint. He knew nothing bad. He didn't know what an obscene word was because he never heard one. If he had heard my father swear, he had forgotten. All he knew was church, because he was pushed to church every day.

I suppose when one starts to write an autobiography, childhood has to be mentioned, or does it? The most important thing without a doubt when writing a book is to write the truth.

In Athens several years ago an American teacher told me about a writer called Genet. He described him as one of the greatest contributors to literature. Had I read his works? As a result I read *The Thief's Journal.* Being an ex-thief, naturally I am always interested in other thieves, just as painters are interested in Rembrandts or Goyas. Because they have also been students and served an apprenticeship. One experience Genet wrote about was how he picked up a Police Chief Inspector in the back streets of Marseilles and buggered him. It always tickled my fancy and amused me, but I couldn't possibly see how this made him a great writer at the time.

I suppose I was about thirteen when the policeman in uniform became my natural enemy. I never knew much about detectives, but I knew the man in blue was the man I had to watch for when I was stealing anything. Squad cars and plain-clothes men on patrol never took much notice of a kid like me.

I did my father an injustice when I said he didn't work. He

did work once a year. Every Christmas he took a job as a temporary postman. His job was to deliver the mail, but the only place he'd deliver it to was home. In he'd come, drunk, with the Christmas mail across his shoulder. I spent most of my Christmas ripping up the letters and throwing them into the fire.

When I was fourteen or fifteen I suggested to him, "Dad, why don't you get yourself a job?"

"Job? Are you telling me to get a job, you saucy little bastard?" It was Sunday lunchtime and I was just about to enjoy a piece of roast beef when he lunged at me with a long knife. Fortunately for me it was a thin one, so it bent. I was up and away because you couldn't mess about with him. He was a raving lunatic once he'd done his nut and if he hit you, you went out, spark out. I retreated down the stairs backwards.

"I'll be back one day and if I ever see my mother with a black eye again I'll break every bone in your body." He leapt down the stairs after me, and I tore away out of the house. I didn't have to pack my clothes. I had none, except the suit I stood up in.

I slept in cars, in the back of carts, in railway vans. I slept in a doss house at a shilling a night with big Irishmen who worked hard as navvies for tenpence or a shilling an hour and came in pissed, spitting and coughing all over the place; creep out in the morning; don't let anybody see you; creep into the local pisshouse, have a wash, brush-up, put a scarf on to hide your dirty shirt. If he was a decent kind of fellow, the lavatory attendant would allow you to wash your collar and cuffs and you'd let them dry on you. I found myself a job selling flowers on the kerb; but I'm going on a bit and jumping ahead.

I was also a thief. People often ask me how I started. How does someone become a thief? Maybe unemployment is very high; people cannot get work, so what are you going to do to get bread on the table? There are two ways: thieving or poncing, a choice of two if you're poor.

I used to come home and see my mother crying because my father had nicked her last few shillings from her handbag and gone to the pub with it. She was crying not because she had no money in her purse, but because she had no food for her children. I thought: well, we've got to eat. My brother and sister were physical weaklings, but I was tough and strong as a kid and I could survive if I was to live on porridge for the rest of my life. I had plenty of that in Dartmoor. (In England 'He's just got some porridge' means a man's gone to prison.)

I couldn't bear to see my mother cry, and since we had no food I used to go out and nick some. But I always wanted an excuse. I'd say to my mother, "Did you want any bread from the baker's?" or "Do you want any stale bread?" She'd rake up sixpence. Once I had the shopping bag, once I had the right, the licence with the sixpence to go into a shop, then I used to start thieving. I used to nick the butter, the eggs, the meat, and I'd go back home with my story. My mother would be waiting; she'd ask me where it came from.

"Well, a rich lady down at the mansions asked me to do a few errands for her. She saw the holes in my socks and me holding the arse of me trousers, wearing my sister's shoes, and felt sorry for me."

We used to call Maida Vale, 'the mansions'. All the rich Jewish and business people lived there in those days. You were considered wealthy if you lived in Maida Vale.

I don't remember any middle class in those days. You were either poor or rich. I saw that poverty represented unhappiness, and began thieving. It was instinctive, like going into the water and learning to swim.

I thought my parents were proud of me being a good little tealeaf, but my mother wasn't. She thought I ought to join the Boy Cubs. All they had to do was get me the uniform. Well, the big night came; they found me an old black seaman's jersey patched up with holes, got me a second-hand green pimple cap and along I went to St Vincent's Church with my pimple cap stuck on top of my red carrotty hair. I was a bit plump, and smothered with freckles. When I saw all the nice clean little boys lined up with new hats, scarves and jerseys I felt out of place. My jersey would have fitted Sonny Liston.

After being given the once over by a poofy-looking scout who gave me a pat on my arse, I was sworn in. The headquarters were in the crypt of a church and had a castle dungeon atmosphere.

They had a game called 'Find the Treasure', and on the desk was a miniature chest full of half-crowns and paper money, contributions to 'THE GREAT CAMPING HOLIDAY'. Needless to say, I found the treasure. Mind you, I knew where the scoutmaster had hidden it. When I had it no one found it. I retrieved the contents a fortnight after, but there was a great hoot. The priest came down and said there was a thief amongst us and one of us would go to hell. As far as I was concerned, I was already living in hell anyway.

I became the local artful dodger. I never got caught. On school excursions I always used to sit on my own and not talk. The teachers used to think I was a good quiet boy who sat in the corner thinking, wearing a pimple cap and short trousers. I remember this. I knew full well I wasn't the boy they thought I was, but to look at me you wouldn't have thought butter melted in my mouth.

Done up especially for school excursions I even had borrowed shoes, but at least I went dressed as smartly as anybody else.

When I was about fourteen years old I had my first drink in a pub. It was a Friday night, and I went again on the following Friday and the following Saturday and the following Friday. This went on for a few weeks and then I looked around at all the people drinking and I thought, is this what life's all about? I'm not going to spend the rest of my life looking forward to a Friday and a Saturday and a Sunday listening to all this nonsense; singing and fucking, shouting and fighting; this is not for me. I am going to get out of it. I am going to get some money.

I looked for any means of making money. This got me in bad at school because I went to work on Sunday mornings instead of going to mass. One of my school teachers had a very pretty face and beautiful eyes. She had a fiery temper; she could rave. On Monday morning they checked us for attendance at nine o'clock mass, confession, communion, Sunday school and benediction. "Just a minute, O'Connor, just a minute. What church were you at?"

"Ah, St Vincent's, Miss."

"St Vincent's? I was at nine o'clock mass looking for you; you weren't there."

They discovered I was a liar.

I think my very pretty teacher knew I was heading the wrong way but had a sneaking sympathy for me. I thought she had given me up as a bad job, but throughout my life she was always willing to help and later visited me in Dartmoor.

One day I arrived home and discovered my mother had disappeared. The neighbours told me she had had another beating.

Then my father disappeared. I was on my own and very worried about my mother. I decided to pack my belongings and try to find her. Just as I was leaving, my father arrived home drunk. I told him where I was going.

"I'm going to look for Mum."

"I'm not stopping you, son."

I was gone. I found my mother with a scar across her throat. She had tried to commit suicide. My father also found her. We lived together in one room. I made up a bed and slept in the passage. It's not very nice to hear your mother being seduced.

I thought I'd teach my father a lesson one day. A fellow used to come round the streets, driving a horse and cart, screaming out, "Goldfish for old clothes, goldfish for old clothes." My father had a beautiful blue serge suit. Out I went and sold it for two goldfish. There was a bit of a hoot when he came home. He went mad. Anyway, it was down to me when he missed it. I was afraid, but I didn't care. But I felt sorry for the poor goldfish man the following week. There were goldfish all over the street.

I would do anything for a couple of coppers. "Paint your knocker, lady?" I was a beggar and used to walk to Regents Park. "Can you tell me the way home, missus? How to get to Hampstead." They would tell me the number of the bus. "I haven't got the fare." They always opened their handbags and gave you a couple of coppers.

I nicked anything I could lay my hands on; always the same old story, "A rich lady from the mansions give it to me."

It was the ox tongue that did it. When I put an ox tongue about three feet long on the table and the old man was there.

"Now don't you tell me that a rich lady from the mansions give you that. Where did you get it from?"

Strange as it may seem, I liked my father. He appeared to be a lonely man. I looked at him and always told him the truth. He trained me to speak the truth, to him at least.

"Nicked it," I said. "Same as all the other stuff. What are you complaining about? What about your pal Charlie the Fish? You're both a pair of thieves. Look at all those hairbrushes. All the backs were stripped off, the gold and the silver. You nicked them somewhere. What about all them gold watches you've been selling with phoney ramps on the chain links that were jars?"

Him and a couple of pals were confidence tricksters in a small way and I told him so. I got a clump and ran out of the house, but he didn't stop me thieving. We eventually became pals and he took nearly everything I stole. I'll never forget walking along Maida Vale with my father and Charlie the Fish; a little boy between two grown-up men. "Now, son," said Charlie, "if you're going to be a thief, be a good one. Never break the eleventh commandment. Never plead guilty, never sign no statement."

My old man was a ham, and very good too. Everybody brought their radio sets to him in those days. It was just after the crystal set had faded out. He always nicked their best parts and would give them back a bit of rubbish. But a better set, anyhow. He couldn't help it. Whenever he wanted anything, he pointed it out in the radio shop window and sent me in. "Go in and get that transformer for me, son." I'd pop in and was very happy to please him. I'd nick it. He was happy. I was happy because I'd made him happy and thought at least Mum won't get a belting tonight. He'll be too busy stripping the wireless set again and putting the new transformer in.

I discovered one other way to earn money was to work. At half past three in the morning I did a milk round for United Dairies. At half past six I'd finish up and do a paper round. At half past seven I'd finish that paper round and do another one. By the time I got to school I was dead tired, always late and in the teacher's bad books. Saturdays I had about five jobs. I worked for the milkman, the butcher, delivered the morning and the evening newspapers, goods from the chemist's. I had a right thieve-up in the chemist's shop. Objects were so small and valuable. I was always loaded when I got home—using my poacher's pockets. It's a wonder that poor chemist never went broke. Anyway, the old man ended up disposing of everything. He used to say, "What have you got today, son?" and I'd have a right unload. He seemed proud of me because I was a good thief.

I left school when I was thirteen. After about a week they tumbled me. They realised I wasn't school-leaving age; no cards. They sacked me. I was better off working at school and had more money than the average working man. Some married men were glad to earn two pounds a week.

Eventually I was taken back to school; the old man took me up to the workhouse and dumped me on the doorstep.

"I can't keep my kid, you keep 'im."

"You must be joking, Dad," I said. "I can keep myself. You think you're leaving me here?"

"Leave off," he said. "Shut up. I'm trying to cop a few bob." And he did—for his poor starving child! He got a bit of beer money and came away laughing; relief tickets, they called them, and worth a couple of quid. You could sell them for thirty bob. The grocery shop would change them, but the shops that took relief tickets would always overcharge the working class. It's always the workers who have exploited the workers.

When I left school my best guv'nors were Jewish people; the kosher butchers and the delicatessens in St John's Wood, Cricklewood, Hampstead and Golders Green, they were my manors. I only stayed with a firm for one day.

"Bicycle boy wanted. Sixteen shillings a week."

A small-front-wheel bike, about a hundredweight of goods in it, slog your guts out pushing it up St John's Wood hills and Hampstead. Jewish people always gave you tips. They were good spenders and spent plenty of money on good food; smoked salmon, gefilte fish, the lot. Of course, they never got all their goods. I used to abandon the bicycle and sell them at my own cut-price store. Unemployed people were pleased to buy them. No questions were asked. I finished up finding a buyer for the bicycle. He used to buy bicycles, save them up and send them down to Kent in a big pantechnicon. They were resprayed, done up, the serial numbers erased and sold back on the London market. It always amused me because he became a respectable member of society.

I often laugh. People think I'm cynical, but I've seen so many people rise from the slums and go into white-collar crime. They're at the top now. They go to Palace garden parties, Ascot, Lord Taverners, golf at Walton Heath and Wentworth. They live in the Surrey green belt. It's a bit different from 1931; the bread line, the dole, relief tickets, rent collectors, tally men knocking on the knocker. "Mum ain't in," was one of the first sentences I learnt. Now, in 1975, I see the '30s again, a nation of fiddlers.

At about this time I fancied getting myself a job as a bellboy on a big liner, P. & O., going to Australia. I had dreams of all types of things, anything to get away from the bugs, but I was unlucky. It was difficult to get a job, so I took the next best thing. I went to a catering labour exchange. They sent me for a job as a pageboy at the Swallow Club, Swallow Street, off Regent Street. Duggie Noone was the guv'nor. I had a job. I enjoyed myself. The hours were late; sometimes I didn't get home till half past one in the morning, six days a week, with half a day off a fortnight and a couple of hours off in the afternoon. But it was a licence; with a uniform and nice white gloves I could walk in anywhere, see a film in the afternoon for nothing, the theatre, variety, anything.

Maserati was the manager of the Swallow Club. Every night he had to have a bowl of minestrone soup, and it always had to come from a special restaurant in Frith Street, Soho. I learned to like minestrone myself, thanks to Maserati. Mind you, he didn't know that I used to eat one-third of the bowl myself and fill it up with hot water. Going backwards and forwards to Soho I used to see the beautiful streetwalkers. The porters told me what type of women they were. I got to know them. They often stood in the doorway of the club out of the rain or to avoid the uniformed policemen who were prowling around.

One night I was walking along Bond Street. I was on an errand for Maserati. It started to pour with rain, so I stood in a doorway and I looked at some of the girls taking shelter. Over in the doorway of Madame Worth's, the furriers, I thought I saw a familiar face; long red hair down to her waist, green eyes, two-piece costume, two silver fox furs, and six-inch high-heeled shoes. I went across the street. It was Saint Anna Maria. That's what I used to call her because that's what she was. Anna Maria was my own mother. A bit flustered, I asked her what she was doing. She told me she was waiting for a bus. Well, I knew the other woman who she was standing with in the doorway. I had seen her pick up her clients. I had always known that there was something wrong in my family. I often wondered why we used to get folding picture cards from Jamaica and sometimes my mother would disappear for a week and there was a great treat when she came home. We had chocolate eclairs from Fortnum & Masons and she wasn't beaten up for a couple of months. When I was eleven, some boys bigger than myself who knew what it was all about called me a few names and said, "Your mother's an whore.' I didn't know what it meant, but I felt it was something unclean. I often used to have to sit outside the house till late at night because I couldn't get in. I used to stand in the doorway of a café across the road. I knew my mother was in our home. I had actually seen her go in with a man. But when I knocked I never used to get an answer. Now I knew why. She was with a client. I found a hole in the wall with a piece of bamboo inserted, camouflaged with a small two-inch piece of wallpaper. When I asked my father what it was for he said it was to run a wire through for an extension speaker, but it looked into my mother's bedroom. It was his Judas hole.

I remember when my mother's sister came round to tell my father that Anna had been arrested for soliciting and was in Vine Street police station. My mother had given her sister's address to protect herself and her children. Later my Uncle Jack, a respectable hard-working man, called round to my father to complain about having his address given to the police. My father knocked my poor Uncle Jack out. He protested what a wicked woman my mother was to do such a thing as this without him knowing. It would have been much better if she hadn't have got bail. He spattered her blood over the kitchen wall, knocked her out for getting caught, and then threw a bucket of water over her to bring her to. Ours was a nice house, ours was—very happy.

My mother was a soft-spoken woman, very quiet and gentle. She didn't go on the streets for pleasure, nor was she lazy. I once asked her why she hadn't left my father years ago. She told me that if it hadn't been for us children she would have done, but who was going to keep us, and wherever she went he would find her. The neighbours were terrified of him. But despite this, I am sure that my mother loved my father because she stayed with him right up to his death in 1950.

My mother's profession has always affected my own private life. During my first marriage, my wife in temper described my mother as an old whore. This hurt me. I slapped her face. A lot of the neighbours knew what my mother did. It's not very easy to keep it a secret when you go out at half past six at night on a Number 6 bus to Bond Street wearing high-heeled shoes and silver foxes. But everybody loved my mother, and always did right up to her death two years ago.

One day I had to take a message to someone's apartment in one of London's most fashionable hotels. While I was there an attractive middle-aged lady gave me sixpence. "Page, take my dog out for a walk." She must have been colour-blind because my uniform was blue and the hotel uniform was green. I took her dog out for a walk as far as Marshall Street swimming baths, the other side of Brook Street where the hotel was, tied it up in the backyard of an Italian café and went swimming for half an hour. When I got back to the hotel I saw all her jewellery lying all over the dressing-room table. That's handy, I thought. I whipped that a bit lively, took the dog out down the trade lift again and went for another walk. In the meantime I hid the jewellery. When I came back the second time it was full of old bill from Vine Street police station. They questioned me. I went straight into my act.

"I'll tell my dad about you. The old girl give me sixpence to take her dog out for a walk; accusing me of things like this!"

Anyway, I heard no more about it. I left the jewellery in a hiding place for about two months. On one of my days off I went home. There was a slight drizzle. We lived in a Portsdown Road church property at Maida Vale. The whores used to solicit outside our door. I slept on the fire escape with two cushions out of an armchair.

Two tall gentlemen with raincoats and caps on were standing outside in a doorway that day. I knew they were old bill; I knew a copper when I saw one.

I went indoors, messed around, poodled about for quite a while, popped along the fire escape, looked over the slanting attic roof. I could see them. They were still there. First of all I thought they were standing out of the rain, but they were still there an hour later. I thought, they're going to give this place a spin. I was worried.

The old man said, "Now what are you doing here? Why aren't you going out?"

"No, I don't fancy going out tonight."

"You must be kidding. You always go skating Fridays."

"Yeah," I said. "But I'm a bit worried tonight about something."

"Come on, what is it?"

"I've got to tell you, Dad, that armchair you're sitting in, now put your hand right down the back."

He did, and pulled out a fruit bag. He took out the jewellery.

"Where did you get this from?"

"I nicked it from Claridges."

"You'll finish up in Borstal, the way you're going on."

"Yeah, if I go to Borstal your pension will go to hell, won't it?"

"Anyway," he said, "now where were these two geezers?"

"In the doorway across the road."

He walked up the fire escape and saw them.

"Ah," he said, "that's nothing. They're watching the place next door."

"What's the place next door?"

"It's a brothel."

I said, "Oh yeah."

Anyway he said, "Now listen; usual routine, out you go, I'll look after this."

He did. The old man was missing for six months; blue serge suits, silk shirts, birds, the lot. I finished up with a toffee apple and a windmill for my whack. He must have had several thousand pounds of jewellery. I didn't know what a brothel was.

I used to have a good run for my money too, but I had the feeling that one day something was going to happen to me that I was not guilty of. I was too lucky as a thief. When I started working with other people, they all seemed to get caught, but I used to fight for it. I'd dive through plate-glass windows, jump over walls, get myself covered in blood and dirt, but I managed to get away.

There's only one thing I ever really regretted stealing in my life. I was working in Glasshouse Street for a Jewish tailor; I used to fell, baste, go to the shops in Savile Row. One day I was diving into his kick. I only wanted a few pounds, but it was loaded. The handle on the door rattled. I didn't want to take the lot, but someone was coming and I panicked. I threw the money under the cuttings, swept them up and took them out in a bag. Whether I liked it or not, I had the lot. I did not know that he was saving up to go and see his son in South Africa. Those were his life savings, but at the time I couldn't think of a way to get them back to him. I was a confirmed thief, and once you steal something you never admit to it and for sure you never give it back. A very famous jewel thief known as 'Taters' in the underworld had a protégé, a nice guy and one of the best jewel thieves in the country—but he was *always* boasting. He couldn't help it. He stole Lauren Bacall's jewels; the newspapers mentioned a brooch that Humphrey Bogart had given her and its sentimental value. The next night he went back to

Belgravia where she was staying, climbed the same balcony and put the brooch back on her dressing-table. Tell no one what you steal, not even the bird you sleep with, the girl you're courting, the girl you're going to marry. Tell no one anything. Admit to nothing. They're going to punish you when they catch you. Thieving's a profession. I've seen many men serving sentences for crimes they didn't commit. Like me, they started thieving in the back streets. The best thieves came from the East End, Hoxton, the Angel, the Elephant and Castle, and, of course, Notting Hill where they had a safe-blowing school. It's thirty years now since I stole anything, but I still think like a thief; the thought of larceny is still there. I have larceny in my heart. I see possibilities missed and anticipate crimes before they're committed. I make crime pay because I write about it.

In those days I never went home without something. I used to nick chickens from the clubs and take them to my mother. My old lady was all right; things were improving; my father seemed to stop knocking her about. He was always complaining of a bad tummy, but would never see a doctor. He didn't believe in them. Said it was the gas from the First World War when he was with the Royal Army Medical Corps, known as 'Rob All My Comrades'. They used to rob the dead when they were lying on the battlefields at Mons and other places. He often showed me his bullet wounds; he put them there himself to give himself a blighty to get home.

"I didn't want any of that nonsense," he used to say. He didn't believe in work, in the State or the Establishment. I can't blame him really. Coming home after the First World War, there was no work for donkey's years. It was worse for unskilled labour. He only had one asset, his good looks. Plenty of women wanted to keep him, and I suppose one or two did when he went missing.

I got a job with the railway as a van boy and met a little gang from Notting Hill Gate. After that I never mixed with the chaps in Kilburn. I emigrated to Notting Hill Gate, and met my first real pal, Bill. He could fight and would never let anybody take a liberty with me. If a policeman started to rough me up during an arrest, then there would be no arrest because Bill would knock him out.

I went to Wembley the night Len Harvey fought Walter Neusel for the championship. It was 1933. All the gang was there. None of us paid to get in. We all gibed, but coming out someone stole a car. I was waiting for a tram when I got a free lift along the Harrow Road. Bill asked to take over the wheel. I didn't know he could drive. I sat in the back. I heard a gong, looked out of the back and saw the illuminated sign, 'Police'. It was a patrol car. The fellow who stole the car jumped out at what we call the Halfpenny Steps, a footpath over the canal. My pal Bill told me to jump. I said I'd stop with him.

"Good," he said. "I'll give the Squad a run for their money." The chase was on. We finished up in a cul-de-sac off the Western Avenue in Acton and the police driver told us we were lucky to be alive. The man who had jumped out of the car was already at Kilburn Police Station when we arrived.

Someone by this time had stuck a knuckle-duster in my pocket which wouldn't even fit my small hand; it was bigger than me. You got nicked for walking home at two in the morning. If you had any previous convictions they would do you for 'Sus'—an unknown charge today. Suspect loitering with intent to commit a felony. You always got a carpet, three months' hard labour. Gawd help us if you were caught walking along Millionaires' Row, The Bishops Avenue, Hampstead.

That was my first charge. I was further charged with possessing an offensive weapon, loitering with intent to commit a felony. I didn't see much 'loitering' at seventy miles an hour. The following morning Bill and I were remanded in custody to His Majesty's Prison, Wormwood Scrubs, for a week.

Poor Bill was in grave trouble because he was already due to appear at the Old Bailey for grievous bodily harm; he was eventually found not guilty on that charge.

My first night in prison was a shock to me. I missed my pal. He was under observation in hospital.

When we came up at Willesden Petty Sessions the third man took the blame for me. I was placed on probation. I went back to my job and got the sack for being a hardened criminal at fifteen.

I became a barrow boy again, selling flowers and fruit. Of course, I fiddled a few bob every day, but I loved selling beautiful fresh flowers. Wrapping them up, I used to stroke them, gladioli like the neck of a swan.

You often got fined for obstruction; ten shillings, two quid, a fiver. If you couldn't pay your fine, you went to jail. I owed about twenty pounds in fines. They came and found me at my mother's. It was snowing. I got out on the roof in my shirt, but they found me. Anyway, it was cold out there. There was no chance of getting my fine paid. I had to do the time in Wormwood Scrubs. By this time I was getting used to prison.

I met a couple of good thieves who were older than me, Joe and Hymie, and had my first experience as a cat burglar. Crooks used to use me because I was little. I could climb through any entrance or small window. They found some old queer who was a butler and used a pub in Mayfair. They knew full well that he had the keys of the safe of her Ladyship's house in Mayfair, and lapped him up and cultivated him in the public bar of what used to be a groom's pub in the old days.

Their job was to get him drunk. My job was to be pushed through a window and lie under the bed in his room until he came in, take the keys from his trouser pocket, let myself out, and hand the keys over to them. The rest was up to them. I agreed to this.

I went to the basement, got in through a small window, found his bedroom and lay under his bed. It was a Sunday night. By the time the pubs closed he was full of pints of bitter. In he came and sat on the bed. He took off one shoe, then threw the other one on the floor; then he threw his trousers across the chair and got into bed. I thought that's it. He'll be asleep in a couple of minutes. I'll be out. I won't take just his keys; I'll take his trousers as well. Suddenly he woke up. I felt a hand coming towards me. He was searching for the piss-pot. I gently pushed it towards him because the bedsprings were tapping my nose by this time. I gave him another ten minutes. He was at it again. By this time it was brimming. Anyway, I managed to get out, taking his trousers and his keys. They did the villainy. I met them the next day when I went to collect my share. All they had found in the wall safe was a row of black pearls which were absolutely impossible to dispose of and a little bit of rubbish. They gave me a couple of quid.

Then I read the newspaper. You can never tell by newspapers because the so-called respectable members of society always inflate the value of stolen jewellery, but the amount was reported as £40,000. There was nothing much I could do about it. They were grown-up men. I challenged them. They denied it and said it was a lot of old nonsense. I asked them where the black pearls were and they told me they had thrown them in the Regents Park Canal. I waited many years to have my pound of flesh, but I had it, because little apples grow and so do humans.

Many years later Joe came into Dartmoor reception wearing a beautiful sixty-guinea suit, silk shirt, the lot. I asked him how long he was doing and heard he had got ten years' preventive detention. He was a tough guy. They put him in a strait-jacket and he could split it with dynamic tension. He had the cat a couple of times.

This is how I had my little revenge. A character was leaving, having served seven years. He had a dodgy old suit from the Discharged Prisoners' Association lot which cost about thirty bob, a crappy shirt, a cheap pair of shoes. I thought, "Well, Joe boy, when you've finished your ten you'll be in for a bit of a shock." I took his beautiful clothes, his overcoat, his crocodile shoes, and changed them into the box of the old lag who was leaving. I bet he did his nut when he went to reception on discharge and opened that old brown box.

You start off by stealing the things that are easiest to steal, from shops when they're alive, from unattended motor-cars. You watch the errand boy fill up with a load of meat or groceries and steal them. And then you say to yourself, "Well, this is a waste of time. I'm a petty thief. This is ridiculous." You read about jewel robberies in the paper and you have the ambition to steal bigger and better things like an actor wants bigger and better parts. Then it's like serving an apprenticeship. First of all I worked alone, but there comes a time when you've got to enter into a certain type of crime, breaking and entering, removing heavy objects, safes, and you have to work with a team, and so you look round to see who you can work with. I joined a team from Notting Hill Gate.

Many good law-abiding citizens admire the Great Train Robbers because they stole two million six hundred thousand pounds. They talk sympathetically about the long sentences they got. A few people in the City and property business, as well as some politicians, should be given a thirty stretch. I have evidence that proves they deserve them.

2

"Let's do a smash and grab"

Half the public were on the breadline at that time, so it soon became known locally that you were a thief because you always had money in your jacket and were smartly dressed. Some people admired you and some despised you out of jealousy. 'Give us a drink', they'd say, and you poured out the gin and lime. My first motor-car cost me exactly one pound ten shillings, and disregarded all laws; no insurance, no tax, no driving licence. They used to call it the Fire Engine. It was a red T-type Ford.

Before I got the motor-car I said to my team, "Why don't we do a smash and grab? You keep hearing about smash and grabs in Regent Street. Let's do a smash and grab."

They'd never done one.

"Well," I said, "there's always a first time. Let's fucking well do one. I'll do it."

And they said, "Where?"

"Well, let's have a look round." So we looked at a couple of jeweller's shops. I found one and said, "That's the one. I'll do that."

"Right," they said. "And what are you going to use for transport?"

"I'm going to do something different. Go round to Billy the Bear's and get a pony and cart. Get Betsy," because Betsy was a fast pony. "And a small cart that can get through a narrow alleyway."

It was a November evening, murky, foggy, and I chose to do it just before the shop closed. The rest of the gang were walking about on the pavement thinking I wasn't going to do it. Betsy was waiting on the kerb with her cart behind her like an impatient burglar. It was past her bedtime. The gang walked up and down nervously.

I walked up to the window and went crash and knocked the

window out and most of the jewellery into the shop. I took the first tray, which was full of poxy rings worth two or three quid, jumped on to the horse and cart, tore up Bosworth Road, leapt out at the Halfpenny Steps and over and away. Betsy cost seven and sixpence a day and we finished up with a tray of rings to share amongst five or six people. No one had done anything except myself, and when we shared it out we virtually had nothing between us.

Then we went to the receiver.

"That one's no good," he said, and threw it into the fire. "That one's all right; that one's no good, that one's no good." We didn't know that after we'd gone he'd rake the rings out of the fire because you can't damage the diamonds, only the shanks. As youngsters we were really in his hands because we knew nothing about the value of diamonds or rubies.

"That's not enough." If you didn't take his money and went away, you found yourself nicked because he would shop you. Most receivers were informers as well. So you would take his money. It took me years to find out all this, but I learned the hard way. You get taken on, twisted, fucked, and then you're accepted as a thief. People start putting propositions to you; they come up and ask you if you've got anything; shopkeepers ask you; greedy people ask you. Just after I first started a woman came up to me.

"Ssss!" I looked round. She had an apron round her money pockets. "Ginger, if you get a single stone, decent size, I'll always have a trade."

"Yes," I said, "I'll bear you in mind. Eventually I jarred her up, just sold her a jargoon, which is a piece of glass. I learnt from other people's greed. I would go to Houndsditch to buy a hundred pounds of shirts, thirds or seconds. They cost me about one-and-six or one-and-nine. I took them back to a receiver as stolen goods at five shillings a time. I had a mug buyer. As far as I was concerned, receivers were criminals as well. They were buying stolen stuff. Everyone seemed to want something cheap, and the poor were getting poorer. Thousands were marching from Jarrow to London.

Eventually I sorted the wheat from the chaff and one day I met two professional criminals who were old lags, which meant they had served a sentence of at least three years; they were grown-up men.

I saw a car full of furs parked at the top of a hill. I used to do car doors with a box spanner. I tried them first of all, then gave them a quick upper and downer; the lock was knocked off. As I was getting into this motor-car two gentlemen came up.

"What are you up to?"

I couldn't drive very well. I thought, I'm nicked. One of them said, "Go on, get in, son," and pushed me over. The other one got in and drove the car. I didn't even know them. We drove round to a lock-up garage in Maida Vale. They went away, sold all the furs and gave me my share. They didn't cheat me.

"Yeah, you're a bit fucking slippery," they said. "We've been watching that lot for three months. You just walked straight up to it."

I had just met two of what are known in the profession as 'jump up merchants'. The 'jump up' is when you follow a commercial vehicle carrying goods or a commercial traveller's car carrying furs or samples of jewellery. I started to work with these two characters. They were both very smart, well-dressed men and we used to go to the City. They knew from experience if something was going to be a bit sticky, so if they needed someone who was quick and good at the 'jump up', they'd say, "We'll be at so-and-so."

They'd point out a box full of silver or gold for the chalice-makers at the back of a cart, and we'd follow it until the horse stopped. I'd go up to the horse and undo its bit, then I'd go round to the van boy.

"Sonny, your horse's bit is undone."

The kid would leave the back of the van to go and put the horse's bit back in his mouth. Of course, you were up into the van, copped the box, into the car and away into a run in, one of several garages rented at ten or fifteen shillings a week in different districts. If you committed a crime in one district you had a lock-up there and didn't have to drive through London with police messages flying backwards and forwards.

When I was about sixteen I met my first wife. I'd turned up being a barrow boy and was now a professional thief. There was no going back. However, she came from a respectable family, bookmakers, bricklayers and builders. They lived in quite a nice district. She was twenty-one. I was sixteen. One day she told me she was in the family way. We were going to get married anyway sometime, so I went up to see the old man and my mother.

"Dad, I'm going to get married," I called up the stairs.

"No you fucking ain't."

"I've got to. I've put a girl in the family way." Anyway, I had the form with me for him to sign.

"I'm not signing that," he said. "Anne, come in here." He called my mother in. She looked sad and asked me who the girl was. I told her. She remembered seeing her on one occasion.

"I can't sign that form, son," she said, "unless your dad says so."

"All right," I said. "Don't worry about that, I'm getting married in the morning, special licence."

"What do you mean, special licence?"

"I'm out on bail, I've been nicked at the jump up. The buyer shopped me."

I'd been nicked in the Edgware Road for stealing a carton of cigarettes from a railway van.

It was a strange wedding at Willesden Registry Office. I'd given a copper the money I had to get bail and promised him another fifty quid which I couldn't get unless I had bail and did a little bit more thieving. I didn't have much time though. We went to Willesden Registry Office on Sunday morning. I had no best man. I saw a little Jewish man with his skull cap on. I called him across the road.

"Guv'nor, do me a favour. Be my best man."

"Of course, laddie, of course."

In he came. I had seven-and-sixpence in my hand. I had to give it to the registrar. After he married me we shook hands and, being an old barrow boy, the three half-crowns were still glued to my thumb and palm.

We got the Number 1 bus back to Kilburn; no wedding reception, no flowers, nothing. I said goodbye to her and she went back to her parents. I was appearing in court in the morning. I got hard labour. "See you when I come out, sweetheart."

I went straight to the pub with the seven-and-sixpence. I earned a few quid that night from a bit of gear I'd stolen. The pub door opened, and in came the relations.

"Here, you," said a gruff voice, calling me outside, "You married my sister."

"Yeah," I said. "What are you going to do about it?"

"Listen," he said. "There's going to be some trouble over this."

"Listen," I said. "I've been in trouble all my life. I'm not worried about you little lot." I went back to the pub.

My pal Bill was there, and said, "What's the matter? Shall I knock them out?"

"No, no, leave them."

At night time back in the pub again, seven o'clock, more relations were there, scowling at me. One of them gave me a big clump with her big crocodile handbag, but they had to face the fact that their relation, their daughter, their sister, was married to me. One of them called me to one side.

"Where are you going to live?"

"I don't know and I don't care."

They didn't know, of course, that I was out on bail.

"Well, come home with us tonight." My wife was there in the background, and she nodded pleadingly to me to make the peace. It was very strange. I went home and stood on the door-step. I heard a voice saying, "I'm not having that thieving whore's son in here." My mother-in-law was pacifying him. I had never met her, but I noticed she had diamonds and big gold rings on.

Straight in; he looked at me, the old man, as though he wanted to kill me. I had taken their only daughter. My mother-in-law showed me to my single bedroom and my wife to her's. They must have been joking.

In the morning a voice shouted, "Are you up there, Jim?"

I thought, "Hello, we've got to the Jim stage already after only twenty-four hours. He would have knocked me out yesterday."

"Yes, I'm up all right."

"Well, get your clothes on, put some old ones on."

"I haven't got any old ones. I only wear new ones. What for?"

"You're coming to work for me."

"You must be joking, coming to work for you. I'm at the sessions this morning."

Anyway, I had a bit of luck. I got a short sentence, but I was a bit disappointed when I was released from prison not to see my wife outside. After all, I loved her in a strange way and she introduced me to sex. I went to my wife's mother's and found her there. She told me she had got a flat for us for about half a quid a week and had furnished it. She pleaded with me to go straight and get a job, so I got one.

I was a hod-carrier, gave my age as twenty-one, wore two coats to make me look bigger, and used my old man's insurance cards. He had cards but never worked. The foreman, to whom I had given a couple of quid, sacked someone else to give me a job. Nice, I thought, but it caused a strike. By six o'clock the following day there were seven sites out and two thousand men marching to Hyde Park in support of the strikers. All because she wanted me to go straight.

While the strike was on I sat about in the canteen. I asked the man behind the counter how much he earned. He told me and I decided to become a catering manager. I faked references and got myself a job as assistant manager in the West of England. I got on the back of a lorry and arrived in the town of Swindon. After a month they made me manager. I was very good at my job. I've always been a good worker when I'm working, but I suppose, like my father, I'm not too keen on it.

Back in London on my weekend off, I discovered that my wife had left the flat we had and the furniture was gone. I always remember her because she left a piece of cheese on a plate near the hole where the mice came out to feed themselves; no bed, nothing, but that was no problem to me.

No crooked man should ever marry a straight, clean-living woman, but in spite of lots of bad things said about them, they are very loyal and will stick to their man. If he sinks to the gutter, they will sink with him, sometimes suffering hardship for many years.

My wife was a very honest woman. She worked hard all her life and still does. One Christmas I was broke and couldn't buy her a present, so I stole a mink coat. I got home at three o'clock on Christmas morning and threw the coat on the bed. She accused me of being out with a bird. I told her I hadn't and that I'd been out to get her a Christmas present.

"I don't want anything that was stolen."

"What do you mean, stolen? I bought it for you."

"What? Bought it at three o'clock on Christmas morning?" And she threw it back at me.

The visiting boxes of any London prison on a Saturday afternoon tell a story; mothers and wives in poor circumstances, visiting the son or the husband who is ashamed of being poor and has been boasting about his wealth to his fellow criminals.

My son was born in September 1936, James William O'Connor. I decided to work again. I worked hard as a labourer carrying a hod with bricks up and down ladders. I got home and gave my wife two pounds ten out of two pounds fifteen wages. After buying myself a packet of Woodbines and a couple of drinks I was broke again on Friday. I used to look at that five shillings and think, 'Well, if that's the result of honesty, long live crime.'

I came home one night and found my wife had left me again. A woman in the flat below told me she had gone back to live with her mother and taken my son. I sold up the second home I had made, despite the fact that it was on hire-purchase, and decided I was going to make as much money as possible and never again get myself mixed up in squalor and poverty for a dollar a week; no more blood, snot, bugs, mice, and lice in my head.

I managed to get hold of fifty quid one night which I didn't have to share with anyone. I spent thirty pounds on clothes, dressed myself up like Farmer Giles and went off to the West Country. I liked the West Country. I stayed at a decent boarding house, bought myself a car in Newbury and drove out to my job every day. I met a very beautiful country girl and she introduced me to all the beauty of the countryside. I always remember her simplicity and sense of humour. I think I fell in love for the first time. The girl had a daughter by me; she knew I was married but separated from my wife. My daughter looked like my sister Kitty who died.

I went back to London and ran into my wife. Once again she wanted me to return to her. I did, for the third and last time. There was no work in London, and it was very difficult. The only entertainment was the local pub, Sunday night fights and drunken brawls. I still wondered about life and thought there must be something better than this, but I was not educated. I just wondered and wanted to know more.

After setting up a home for my wife, the money I had saved and nicked soon began to disappear. I went after a job, but so did thousands of others. I had a car and decided I was going to be a full-time crook.

3

Corporal James O'Connor 10539

In September 1939 when the sirens went, I decided to join the Air Force. I went along to Acton Recruiting Office with a couple of local bookmakers. They were accepted; I was rejected. They told me to wait till I was called up. I thought it was a funny old war. I wanted to join it and they didn't want me.

Walking through a street in Paddington, I ran into a boxer who was in army uniform.

"Hello, Freddie boy," I said. "When did you join up?"

"Last week. Why don't you join my mob?"

"What's your mob?"

"Royal Army Service Corps, E.F.I."

"What's that stand for, E.F.I.?"

"Expeditionary Forces Institute, NAAFI."

I went to the Imperial Court, Kensington. I was on my way to fight Hitler, but after a bit of advice I took a job as a chargehand which automatically made me a full corporal.

I went to Sutton recruiting depot, took the oath of allegiance and went up to Croydon to get fitted up with khaki. Someone gave me two chevrons and said I was a corporal, the most unworthy in His Majesty's uniform. Another fellow gave me a gun, a ticket for a billet, AB 64,* and a ration book. I studied the book-keeping system of the NAAFI for a couple of days. Someone said, "Corporal James O'Connor 10539, report for musketry drill." I gave the fellow a nicker and got myself a couple of days' leave instead.

The old man went mad when he saw me khaki.

"I'll chop your fucking arm off before you leave England. Joining the army! You should be ashamed of yourself."

He nearly went into convulsions when I said I'd given a fellow

* Soldier's paybook.

five pounds to put me on first draft overseas. I told him my plans and said once I had studied the catering game I could get a commission in a few months, with a bit of string-pulling. I had joined to thieve, not to fight. All the wide boys thought I had gone mad when they saw me in khaki.

At Millbank they injected me with a serum which gave me forty-eight hours' leave before leaving for France. On parade before going on leave, we were inspected by a pukka colonel and, presenting arms, I lifted up the rifle and put it on my shoulder. With no training, I think I did very well, but the colonel was shocked when he saw a corporal who could not present arms. He had me fall out in the square, and detailed a sergeant to teach me the rudiments of musketry. In spite of that, after ten days in Kate Carney's army I was bound for France, dreaming of all that crumpet and all those beautiful French girls I was going to have. My father and my uncles had talked about them.

Apparently I was on punishment, so I had to look after all the other officers' kit, which ironically improved my position. Going across I had a cabin of my own. I had a couple of pals aboard. They piled into the cabin and we had a little party until we docked at Le Havre.

I had to take the officers' kit ashore, put it on a wagon and take it to the billet. I asked one of the officers how I was to get there.

"Well," he said, "just ask the first person you see."

Those NAAFI char wallahs were living like lords, but they had one big moan about being in France for three months; they were not working in canteens as they had been recruited for. I asked what they were doing for duties and they complained of unloading shiploads of supplies at the docks, storing the supplies at the warehouse and distributing them to various sections of Northern France.

At six o'clock the following morning we paraded outside the billet, knife and fork in hand, and marched with our mugs to another building in the Rue Victor Hugo to the chorus of "Roll out the barrel". After a hearty breakfast the order was issued, "Corporal J. O'Connor, report to warehouse for duty."

When I arrived at the warehouse it was like going into a jail; big iron gates and soldiers on guard. Inside were shipments of millions of pounds of tobacco lying all over the place. Some of it was covered with snow outside the warehouse. It didn't matter.

There was plenty. I immediately thought of the mugs who were working there, and realised that they were mostly straight, honest men who were being employed by Joe Lyons, Thomas Lipton's Tea Shop, the Express Dairy, and had been employed for many years by the NAAFI.

The place was lousy with French stevedores, a real tough-looking mob of apaches. I was put in charge of a gang of Froggies in the tobacco and spirit store. I knew that somehow I was going to make a lot of money despite those iron gates. At night I went round Le Havre sightseeing. I was taken into the brothels about which journalists are always writing exposés, saying, "When asked for money, I left." Up your nelly. I didn't either. I had a few right downers. Their mothers must have given them tuition when they were thirteen years of age. They were very attractive girls, irresistible. I didn't feel ashamed. I was twenty-one.

In one brothel I saw an exhibition between two lesbians and two young prostitutes. I've seen worse in sexy shows in London's West End. I have an open mind on sexual behaviour. I don't hold a brief for sexual degeneracy, but I've seen so much of it in my life I consider it a form of mild abnormality.

On the following day I got down to business and decided I needed help. Having watched the Frenchmen petty thieving for twenty-four hours I knew I wouldn't have to look far, but I wanted the right men. The Frenchmen were either good or bad thieves, but there was no doubt they were all thieving. I found a Frenchman speaking English to one of the soldiers. It came about that he had worked at the Savoy Hotel in London. That's very interesting, I thought. I took him into the office, opened a case of whisky, got friendly with him, and soon discovered he was a member of the Parisian underworld. He had moved up to Le Havre to see what he could plunder and had got himself a job inside the warehouse to case the joint for the firm he was working for.

The following night, dressed in mufti, I was picked up by a car and taken to a low-down dockside café, out of bounds to troops. I could not talk very well to my waiter's mates. He said a few words. I was greeted and shook hands with half a dozen men and women who did not like shaking hands with strangers. It was not their custom. They told me to go down to a more exclusive part of the town until Joseph arrived.

Joseph did arrive. He was the guv'nor and spoke a little English. They took me to a nightclub and it turned out that Joseph was the owner. They put a proposition to me. At the back of the warehouse was a great big sliding door, the key to which was kept in the lodge by the gatekeeper, but they had obtained an impression. So far they had been unable to do anything because of the guard at night. I told them to leave it to me. If they had a key, I had a better way than that. In a few days we could take out a fifteen-ton load in broad daylight at least once a week; at least that's what I thought, but the following morning I got a shock: the roster. It was my turn to be Corporal of the Billet for one month. I was taken off warehouse duty. I didn't mind really because at this time I had plenty of money, plenty of scratch and all the time in the world; just sit there and book the mugs out.

Next door to our billet in Rue Victor Hugo was a brothel; beautiful birds, a beautiful building with a slanting attic roof and open french windows. The darlings used to tease us while they sat on the balcony, but they were a bit too expensive for some of our troops and I decided that I only wanted a girl on my merits. I was vain and played hard to get, just sitting at that door.

There was no discipline. We didn't know what it was. It was like Kate Carney's army, and anyway they weren't any good to the girls next door. Half of them were poofs. One night I discovered a bit of a noise going on at the top of the billet. I went up. There they were, sheep's muslin dyed, women's dresses, lipstick, dancing, kissing each other. This was the British Army—so-called His Majesty's. On this particular occasion it looked more like Danny La Rue's. There was only one thing I could do.

"Get them fucking clothes off."

I made out that the Commanding Officer had paid us a surprise visit—inspection. There was one mad rush. I nipped down the stairs lively, laughing to myself. Gawd help us if they're going to fight the Germans, I thought, or maybe they're going to fuck the Germans!

But while I was at the billet I made quite a few discoveries. Lots of new faces had arrived, but this time it wasn't Joe Lyons. It was faces from Pentonville, and Wandsworth Jail. We'd all been in the nick together in England. It was handshakes all round.

I took them into my little quiet café. Madame was a beautiful aloof silver-haired Frenchwoman. She was my friend, crooked as arseholes, and would do anything for money, but she was honest as far as I was concerned because at this stage she was looking after my money. Every time we had a count up it was always there, not a penny missing. Mind you, I wasn't subtracting; I kept adding, and she went short of nothing, nor did half that street; cases of eggs, sides of bacon, tinned hams, plenty of whisky, plenty of English cigarettes. All the villainy took place there.

The first one I saw was Mad Smithy. As he walked into the billet I greeted him, "Hello, Smithy boy, when did you come out?"

He looked at me. He was shocked, and whispered, "Don't let anybody know about me."

"You must be joking. I need you."

The next one was Geordie, also mad and known as "Mad Geordie". He had a big indentation in his forehead and he could fight. There was a well-known boxer from Fulham and a couple from my own district, Kilburn, Paddington.

I would say those few months in France must have been one of the happiest times in my life; so much so that I refused to come home to England on leave and gave it to a man who had a wife and four kids.

But things didn't always go smoothly. I was sitting at the table on the door of the billet one day. Two sergeants came along.

"Corporal James O'Connor, 10539."

"Come inside." They took me inside. "Where's your locker?"

"Over there."

"Where's your bed?"

"Over there."

Being an N.C.O., I shared a room with another N.C.O. We did it in shifts—four on, four off. I showed them my locker.

"What are you looking for, mate?" No answer. "What are you looking for, mate?" No answer.

"Turn out your pockets." In my pockets I had a wallet, a few registered letters from my father, a photo of my wife and baby, a picture of my girl from the West Country and our baby, a few francs, a couple of English pound notes and a Scottish fiver, but of course by searching in such a fashion they'd marked my card.

"Right," they said. "Lead on, headquarters."

Headquarters was two blocks away from the billet. They walked along the street, one each side of me.

"Listen," I said. "Walk behind me. Everybody knows me in this street. Don't worry, I'll go down the HQ. I don't need your help."

It was a joke because if they had been pukka army sergeants they wouldn't have stood it.

"Now fuck off," I said. "Otherwise I'll chin the two of you."

I don't know which one of them worked for Joe Lyons, but they were in a bit of a state and they did walk behind me, but we had to pass my little café. I popped in quickly and told Madame Samuels there was a bit of bother. I didn't know what it was all about, but not to worry, I'd be seeing her; look after the boodle, the money.

When I arrived at headquarters, sitting behind this great big oak desk in his palatial office was a little tiny man about four foot eight. I suppose he must have been the managing director of Sainsbury's or something, playing the part of a Commanding Officer. It was a real joke. When he spoke his little squeaky voice said, "Corporal James O'Connor, 10539."

"Yes, sir."

"Well—em, em—now let me see. Yes—er—yes—er—well, I tell you what we wanted to see you about. We've had one or two complaints that, you know—you've been going about on your own in the city. Are you aware of the fact that troops must move about in pairs? Four or five of our boys have been found stabbed; two or three killed and their bodies thrown in the Seine."

"Yes," I said, "I'm fully aware of that, sir. Yes."

"Well, in future you will always travel accompanied by someone else."

"Well, I have no desire to be with anybody else except a girlfriend." I was courting a girl from the Monoprix, a cashier, a very nice and beautiful girl. We were enjoying life and had the best of everything. Unfortunately, I had been seen by officers in the best places, paying bills for maybe more than they earned in a month. The girl wasn't taking me out. She wasn't a prostitute; she was a worker. We were just enjoying life. Anyway, I said to the Commanding Officer, "Is that all you want me for, sir?"

"No," he said. "We've been told that you've been spending large sums of money."

"Quite right. I don't know about large sums of money, but I suppose you know my father happens to be a very rich man. He's a bookmaker in London and if you look in my wallet that those two sergeants have got wrapped up in the *News of the World* you'll see registered letters from my father."

By arrangement, my father had been writing me letters: "Dear Son, enclosed is £200, £300." Christ, he'd never given me two bob in his life.

"I happen to be a gambler, sir, like my father, and I've been running the crown and anchor."

"Well, you know it's not allowed, Corporal."

"I know, sir, but it's better than being in brothels."

"Yes, lad. Well, I don't want any more of that."

"Sir, it's not what you want. It's what I want. We came here to fight the Germans. I'm fed up with this Kate Carney's army. I'm going to let the national newspapers in Great Britain know all about it. And you're the Commanding Officer in charge of poofs dressed up in cheap mutton cloth and lipstick. Have they come to fight the Germans or fuck them? I want a transfer. I want to be in a fighting unit. I want to go to Narvik, anywhere I can fight the Germans. I'm not going to sit on the door like a spook each day counting this lot of poofs in and out." That's one way of getting back to the warehouse, I thought.

"I want to do something physical, sir. I can't stand this, etc., etc. I am writing to the British newspapers. I'll let them know in Great Britain what's going on."

He changed his tune a bit towards me. I had upset him, touched him on a sore point. After all, he was the Commanding Officer and it was a bloody good story for the newspapers. I had no intention of giving it to them anyway.

"What's more, sir, if you don't take me away off this billet duty, working for all these poofs, I shall write to the Minister of War as well."

He hummed and hawed for a couple of minutes and then said, "Right, stay another two or three days, and then back to the warehouse. By the way, Sergeant, there's been some misunderstanding here. The Sergeants were not instructed to search you or arrest you."

"They treated me like a prisoner, sir; walked me along the

pavement, one each side of me. Did you call me Sergeant, sir?"

"You've been recommended to be a sergeant."

"Oh, thank you."

"In the meantime you'll be acting sergeant."

"Oh, thank you, sir. That's very nice of you."

He's done a right Edgar Wallace here, I thought. That newspaper story came in handy. He got me here to try and find out where I got my money from.

"Give it a few days and you'll be back at the warehouse. Yes, we're making you a sergeant of the police."

Christ, I thought, me a policeman. This *is* a joke.

"Your promotion will be confirmed in a few weeks from London."

Well, I was happy about that. I knew my wife's allowance at home would be increased, although she didn't need it because I was sending her plenty of money home. I had many ways of sending it home, stuffed inside dolls and toys and various presents I gave soldiers to deliver. They never knew they were delivering money; nor did the people in England know what was inside the presents. My only worry was that all the presents would be there when I got back, if I ever got back.

I went back to the billet for a couple of days, and then a bomb hit us; a bomb in the form of a regimental sergeant major, pukka army, from the Brigade of Guards, who had been sent across from England to put us through disciplinary measures. When he arrived at the billet door, tall, ginger-haired, with a big moustache, and a baton at his side, my tunic was undone; I was wearing a khaki silk shirt, hand-made shoes and a tailor-made uniform. I had three stripes by this time.

"Sergeant."

"Yes, guv. What do you want?"

"Don't call me 'guv'. You call me sir, SIR, SIR, SIR, SIR!"

"Nobody calls anybody sir here. What do you want, mate?"

It was just like *The Army Game*. He couldn't believe it.

"Stand to attention when you're talking to me."

I reluctantly stood up. I don't think I was capable of standing to attention. I sat on the edge of the table.

"Now before you start barking and shooting your mouth off, will you just listen to me. And tell me who you are and what you are." He told me what he was and went to inspect the billet. All the men were out at work. None of them had made their beds up. He was doing his nut, so I started to do my chatting up bit and fall in line bit. He saw the state of their beds, their rifles smothered in dust, and then he asked to see my rifle. Well, I really didn't know what a 'pull through' was. I'd never used one. I'd never fired the rifle in my life. I had a couple of .45s I wasn't supposed to have, but they were tucked away. He was in a bit of a state. He couldn't nick me. He needed me. I made out that it was someone else's rifle and that my breech block had gone and was at the armoury. He stood for that one; he wanted to anyway.

He was a right bastard. When the boys arrived back at night time he had them all lined up and gave them a right talking to. One or two cracks were coming from the old lags. I thought, he'll enjoy himself with this little team.

He showed them how to make their beds up and went away. That's got rid of him, I thought. Then the cunning bastard came back at about half past twelve. Everybody should have been in the billet by ten o'clock, but there were still at least twenty-five empty beds. The boys were in the brothels or dodging the red-caps, working their way back to the billet. Fortunately I was sitting reading a book, just waiting, biding my time to get back to the warehouse.

"Right, I want to inspect the troops."

They were lying about pissed all over the place. He saw the empty beds and just sat and waited.

As they came in, "Sergeant, local garrison"; "Sergeant, local garrison." Half of them were my pals.

I said, "Sir, I've got news for you. We've got no local garrison. We've got a room upstairs, that's all."

"Right, pick up your blankets and take them upstairs." There wasn't even a lock on the door. I had to tie it up with a piece of string. Needless to say, they didn't spend the night there. They were out of the french windows, along the attic roof and into the brothel. I said, "Be back in the morning, boys."

Then I took the sergeant major downstairs; I still couldn't break him : well, he'd come to break us.

"Now listen," I said. "I've got news for you, mate."

"Call me sir," he said.

"I'm calling you mate. Let's put our cards on the table. You are a pukka British Regimental Sergeant Major, right?" That, he agreed to. "I suppose you spent all your life in the army, right? These people have spent half their life in the Home and Colonial, Joe Lyons, Sainsburys. They've had no training, nothing at all. Within one hour they might all be called out of bed again to unload a ship, thousands of tons of ships are coming in; unloading so the Germans can't bomb them as sitting ducks. Their wages—they have AB 64 but you'll find pages missing from the middle. We are civilians in uniform. We are not soldiers of His Majesty's Army. We are paid the same wages that we would be paid if we were the NAAFI working in England. The only difference is that we've got uniform on. I've got stripes. You've got a crown on the sleeve of your jacket and all you're heading for is plenty of trouble."

There was still one bed empty. He wanted to know the name. I told him I couldn't tell him; we'd lost the book. I knew who it was: Geordie. He never came home till five or six in the morning if he had a bird. But this bastard, he waited. I thought you'll be lucky.

"Now listen," I said. "There's a party working at the docks."

"I have inspected the guard at the warehouse. There is no one missing there."

"Oh."

He waited until Geordie came back pissed. You can guess the rest of the story. When he asked him to call him sir, Geordie said, "Get fucked," chinned him and knocked him out. It was the first time one of our men had been arrested by the redcaps.

"Don't worry, Geordie boy," I said. "I'll be round there in the morning to see the Commanding Officer."

The following morning I made a visit to the Provost Marshal's quarters, asked to see the Commanding Officer and was taken in front of him. I put the case of the civilian worker and said they had no authority whatsoever to arrest a civilian. He paid National Insurance stamps and earned a wage. If he looked inside our AB 64s he would see that the pages were missing. It stated what we were recruited for: chargehands, canteen managers, assistant managers, assistants, supervisors, checkers, storemen. The billet was a transit billet where men were waiting to go to various parts of France to carry out the jobs they had been employed for and recruited for by the NAAFI in England, perhaps from the Home and Colonial Stores. I repeated the same story I had already told the sergeant major. These men weren't recruited to unload ships while being machine-gunned and bombed by German planes over the docks at Le Havre.

"Without any hesitation, sir, these men are ready to go out at any time of night and unload ships. They could quite legally refuse. That's for the troops to do."

I informed him that in the event none of these men had ever been informed that they came under the military police, that they had had no training and didn't know how to use a gun. He couldn't believe me when I told him.

He scratched his head. I gave him the newspaper story. I told him I myself wanted to go away and fight the Germans. Deep down inside I hoped I never ever saw one.

Anyway, he didn't charge Geordie Johnson; under the circumstances he dropped the charge against him, told me nobody was to leave the billet that night, called in to see us all and gave us a talking to. Everybody was confined to the billet and he sent Geordie Johnson back to England. I saw him a couple of years afterwards, just after I had been reprieved. He was doing eighteen months for blowing a safe.

I returned to the billet and was informed that I was relieved of my duties. The following day I was to report to the warehouse. This made me very happy. I had a day off, went out shopping and bought myself some new underwear. At the Monoprix I saw my sweetheart and told her the good news; the billet duties had interfered with our evenings out; four hours on, four hours off, four hours on.

When I returned to the billet with my shopping the place should have been empty except for the sergeant on the door. I walked down the flight of stairs and heard someone crying. I looked over the staircase; it was two soldiers kissing each other goodbye. I couldn't believe my eyes. One of them had been transferred to Arras. They were sweethearts being parted from each other. I thought gawd help us if the Germans ever get here.

The following day I reported at the warehouse, Acting Sergeant James O'Connor in charge of the police. Well, I selected my own police force. Of course, they were all my own pals. The Froggies used to knock off work round about half past eleven. They would line up and we used to spread out across the cobbled street running through the middle of the warehouse and rub them down and search them. It was ironic; all of us had been rubbed down so often in the nick in the past. A couple of mugs were foolish enough to be caught with something on them; they had many other ways of getting stolen stuff out without carrying it on their bodies.

There was an officer over me, but he stayed in the office most of the time. Very, very reluctantly we had to take one into him. The French police came and picked him up in a van; right bastards they were. They used to kick them into the van when they nicked them.

During the course of the day lots of stevedores used to break open cases of cognac, get drunk and had to be taken away.

Paddy Burn became my right-hand man. He was a veteran from the First World War and he spoke fluent French. I sounded him out. He put his cards on the table; he'd come there to thieve.

The warehouses were set out A, B, C, D, E, F, G, H, in separate units. Cigarettes were stacked in $3\frac{1}{2}$ cwt cases. It was like walking up the steps of St Paul's Cathedral. Six- and eight-wheeler lorries pulled in from the dockside to the warehouses.

After we rubbed the Frenchmen down our men used to go off to have their lunch. We stayed behind to guard the warehouse; a right lot of guards we were. We were scheming. I had two men in each warehouse.

One day Paddy Burn came back to me.

"Jim, there's something funny going on in B warehouse."

"What do you mean, something funny? There's no one there except Jim and Wally." Wally was the boxer from Fulham.

"Well, come and have a look for yourself."

I went down to B warehouse, walked up the steps of the cigarettes and looked down to a toilet. I don't have to tell you what a French toilet's like, especially on a dockside; just a hole in the ground with a channel running away to the sewage. It was hidden by cases of tobacco next door to the big sliding back gates. I looked down. Lying down was a Frenchman, lying in piss and shit, apparently drunk.

"What's so strange about that?" I said to Paddy. "He's got pissed and the poor fellow's fallen asleep there."

"I saw him just before lunchtime and then he was as sober as a judge."

"We'll just sit here and wait."

We just sat on the top, looking down. All of a sudden up he got, sober as a judge. He went to the sliding doors, inserted a key as big as my arm, and slid them back. In came a covered wagon. Out jumped about eight men with grappling hooks and they loaded up the wagon. It was all done in a few minutes and they were gone. We sat there watching. He locked the door and went back, but not to the toilet. He moved a case. They had stacked the cases in such a way that inside was a room, and this is where he stayed until after lunch. Then he carried on his work.

I thought that's how it's done. Joseph had wasted no time. He'd done without me. Well, I didn't see Joseph amongst the team, but I saw Jean and a black man. He wasn't hard to pick out. After lunch I saw that the black man was one of the workers there. We said nothing.

The following day I got my little team. We hid ourselves. We looked down into the toilet, but there was no Frenchman lying there. That's strange, I thought, and wondered how many times a week they were doing it. What had I been missing by being back at that billet?

We just sat there and smoked. All of a sudden we saw a case move. The Frenchman came out. He repeated the same thing, but this time they had it. We had .45s which we weren't allowed to have, and lined them up against the wall at the end of bayonets. They were scared out of their lives and thought they were nicked.

"Go on," I said to Paddy. "You can speak French. Speak to them. That black man there." He was doing all the shouting and talking. "Shut up, you thieving bastard. Go and stand against the wall."

We had to act a bit officiously. He went to attack me with a grappling hook, but Wally done him with the butt of a rifle and knocked him out. We became friends afterwards.

"Anyway, which of you is the guv'nor here?" Paddy asked them.

"Ask them how much this little lot comes to," I said. Paddy spoke to them in French. Then one of the Frenchmen spoke up. Paddy told him not to worry. They weren't going to be nicked.

"Come tomorrow with bigger lorries." We wanted half of it, our share, in cash, in readies that night, and we wanted the key.

Well, they were so surprised and so happy that they weren't nicked.

"Go on," I said. "On your way. Give us the key. Bring us back the readies."

I picked out two or three faces that worked there and looked at their hands; unsoiled. In actual fact, it turned out they were an organised team from Paris, real professional villains. I decided I'd go with them in case we got caught for our share of the loot.

My pals were afraid they'd kill me, knock me off.

"Don't be silly," I said. "They're not going to kill the hand that feeds them. I'll give Paddy the key. There's a fortune lying here. You must be joking."

I went with them. They drove the lorry out to a roadhouse, a café-cum-restaurant and night club. We went round to the back of it. It was during the day. They had a count up with the amount of cigarettes they'd got, and they knew exactly what it would come to; didn't mess about. Who came out? Joseph; gave me an envelope full of French francs, the largest denominations. They took me back in the Citroën to the warehouse. I knocked on the door; Paddy let me in.

This went on for quite a while. One day we discovered another little firm working there. They had an ingenious scheme for getting the snout out. An engine used to come in, go on to the turntable and turn round. One of the poofs, a storeman on warehouse duty, came and reported that a number of cases were missing from the warehouse. Being a policeman, I had to go and investigate. Well, no sign of forced entry; no broken cases.

"You'll have to check your stock again," I said. "That's all." I knew someone was at it. Paddy and I kept watch on that warehouse. We always wondered why that engine driver had such a nice smile, "Good morning, good afternoon, good evening", all the old cobblers.

He was at it, getting it out in the coal bunker. We copped out of it too. We copped all ways, couldn't go wrong. At any rate, I accumulated plenty of money.

However, all this ended. I tumbled that Security Police Intelligence were being slipped into the warehouses and on to the docks. I recognised a C.I.D. from the Yard dressed in khaki. He was no ordinary NAAFI man. He didn't recognise me. I had time on my side. Fortunately, I never kept any money on me. It was secreted away in different places; Madame Samuel's; my girl had some. I had plenty. By this time I had about £20,000. It was a lot of money in those days. I decided to call it a day. The best thing I could do was get out of that warehouse and get out of Le Havre.

4

Then a dirty big wave came along . . . .

The following day I reported to the Commanding Officer and made a request. If he looked at my AB 64 he would see I had been recruited as a canteen manager and that I had been employed in Britain by John Barker's catering firm. I told him that I had had enough. I would like to go back to my own trade as canteen manager or chargehand.

The following week I was given orders to take a convoy of fifteen lorries to a racecourse called Château Blanc, just outside Rouen, where twenty-five thousand troops were stationed. They had no canteen and we had to erect the biggest under-canvas canteen in France, No. 1 B.D. (Number 1 Battalion Depot).

The Commanding Officer of the camp asked me if I could ease the situation for the troops by erecting our marquee the evening we arrived. He couldn't order me to do it, but he lent me a couple of dozen of an Irish Rifle Regiment; a right load of thieves they were. It was teeming down with rain. We erected a canvas NAAFI for the night; only a makeshift job. My men were moaning and groaning until I pointed out that these men were real soldiers and were going to fight the Germans.

"While they're getting killed we're serving Cadbury's milk chocolate, tea and beer."

I think I won the war on Cadbury's milk bars. Their consciences pricked a bit. We unloaded the lorries and sold out of all the booze, all the ale and stout; no tea that night. We had not erected the kitchen. The following day we did the job properly; hot food and beverages for the lumps and bumps.

I enjoyed my visit to the city of Rouen the following day. I met a very attractive girl called Tania. Her father was Russian; her mother was French. Her parents were in fact living in Algiers.

I met her at a club. Her job was to make the officers spend

as much as they could on champagne. They worked on a commission basis. No doubt one or two of the girls went off on the side, but nothing took place on the premises. A private or N.C.O. had to leave the club at eleven o'clock, but commissioned officers were allowed to stay until midnight.

I used to get a bit jealous when I saw Tania sitting with officers, pouring out champagne, but she used to wink at me because the joke was on the officers. I had the key to her flat. At eleven o'clock I used to go back there and wait. She'd arrive back just after midnight.

I bought myself some civilian clothes and she used to take me to nightclubs tucked away which no officers or redcaps knew about. That hour I used to wait for her served a very useful purpose to me. She gave me an extra key and I virtually moved into the flat. I found a cubby hole which not even she knew and hid my money in her flat. I had the key, the money, the cubby hole. What more did I want? I had no intention of going back to England while the war was on.

I was lying in bed one night with Tania when she asked me to marry her. Oh, Christ, I thought, I should ask my wife in London first of all.

"Of course, darling, of course. With a little bit more time. See what happens with this war."

She suggested we go to Algiers and live with her parents. I thought that's not a bad idea, but I want to get some more money first.

I used to catch a taxi back to camp in the morning at six-thirty. I had no one to account to.

One night while I was waiting at Tania's flat I went to my cubby hole to get my money and add some to it. I got a bit of a shock. It was gone. I switched off the music and waited in silence till Tania arrived with a couple of bottles of champagne. I said nothing. We started drinking.

"Come on, darling, let's go to bed."

I let her get undressed first.

"Come on, darling, where is it?"

"Where is what?"

"Where's my money? Don't mess about."

I got hold of her and tied her to the bed.

"Jimmy, I tell you where the money is when you marry me."

I ripped the flat to pieces. She was like a wildcat. I couldn't find the money. She tried to convince me that she loved me and said she could have disappeared with my money. That was true. I had not told her about my cubby hole; she had found it. I untied her and promised her I would marry her and we would go to Algiers. She seemed happy.

"Darling," I said, "give me the money. I've got some business to do." Still no money.

"Jimmy, I'll give you the money after we've been married."

"Sweetheart, we'll get married tomorrow by special arrangement." She was a Catholic; so was I. I told her I would get the Catholic priest from the base to marry us.

The following day I turned up with the Catholic priest. It was Paddy Burns done up in officer's uniform and dog's collar, and a few pals. We went through the ritual of being married and went off to celebrate in an afternoon club, but first of all we popped back to the flat.

"Tania, come on, my darling. I've a little present for you." I'd bought her a present. I wanted the money. "Come on, darling, give us the money, please." I gave her her present, a black patent handbag with goldleaf. You just turned the top and it opened like a tulip.

There was no money in the flat.

"I won't be five minutes."

Away she went; back she came and gave me a parcel of money. Every penny of it was there. She was very happy. She thought I was her husband and talked about how we'd get to Marseilles and how she'd fix to get to Algiers. She reminded me once again that she could have stolen that money from me any time. We had a right night on the piss.

The following morning we went to get a taxi to go back to camp and found we were in trouble. It was absolutely impossible. The bridge was jam packed. Jerry had invaded the Low Countries.

We sat on the parapet of a bridge in Rouen. For me this was a revelation of what war really meant. Millions of refugees poured over that bridge, the old, the young, the rich, old cars, new cars, just one mad rush, thousands of Belgians among them, little fair-haired children. The French despised the Belgians and would not sell them food. Thousands were gathered in the market square at Rouen. This sight brought tears to my eyes. Paddy and I went to the local warehouse, loaded up with food and gave it to the refugees. When it was all gone, one woman offered her body to me just to feed her children. We took her to a French café. The owner took one look at her and her children and knew they were Belgian. He refused to serve her, but we had a surprise for him. We pulled out a couple of .45s. At gunpoint we made him serve her, then filled her up with as much food as she could carry and said goodbye.

There was a shock in store for us when we arrived back in camp. Four-fifths of the camp was empty. The troops had marched out but their progress was impeded by thousands of refugees. Jerry was machine-gunning them. Apparently the Germans were no more than fifty kilometres away. There were hundreds of vehicles and motor-cycles. No one had set fire to anything. They had just abandoned everything.

A cockney kid and myself took an ambulance loaded up with cigarettes and tins of ham, all the food we wanted, a right load up.

"Right," I said. "The Germans are fifty kilometres that way. We're going *that way.*"

I went into town. The Royal Engineers were the only regiment in the camp when we left. I went to say goodbye to Tania and thought there'll be a right scene here but I'll fanny my way out of it somehow. When I got to the flat she wasn't there. I left her some money and wrote her a note telling her my conscience was pricking me and I was going to fight the Germans up the Maginot Line; I had her parents' address in Algiers and would try and contact her. I told her I loved her.

Then me and this cockney kid left, heading south as we thought. We arrived at the town of Nantes which was a bit further away from Jerry. I was planning on going to Marseilles. We parked the ambulance on the square, and a redcap approached me.

"Jerry's about fifteen kilometres away," I said.

He looked surprised. Anyway, they told us where the nearest R.A.S.C. depot was. There wasn't any arrest.

We reported to the base in town, a warehouse-cum-small barracks. The officer in charge looked like David Niven. He didn't lose any time and gave me a small convoy to go to a camp about fifteen miles north of Nantes where the troops were without supplies, cigarettes, booze and food.

We didn't mess about. As soon as we got there they rushed

us. We didn't bother to erect the tent at all, just put up the tables, unloaded cases of cigarettes, beer and chocolate, and sold as much as we could.

The cockney kid was still with me.

"Come on, Sid, are you going to stick with me? I'm your sergeant." He agreed. "Right, get the lorry out; throw all that gear off. Keep the food, plenty of cigarettes and some booze," and we were away. We headed for St Nazaire. Of course, the kid had no idea how much money I had. I didn't tell him. I'd had a special box made by a blacksmith which fitted inside my valise. It was full of money; French money, English money, Irish money, Scotch money, gold rings, watches, everything, the lot. I had a body belt made to fit, and it had a few thousand francs round it.

Thousands of troops were pouring into the centre of St Nazaire. It was absolutely impossible to drive the vehicle. We had to abandon it and give away the food. We carried as much as we could. Jerry was machine-gunning and dropping out of the sky. It was a very bad night, with plenty of bombing. Unfortunately, I got a splinter of shrapnel in my left forefinger. In no time it turned septic. By the morning my temperature was 102. I walked very weakly along the quayside and saw some officers sitting on some big black boxes. They were NAAFI money boxes. Although I was ill, my brain was still on money, money, money. It's been the curse of my life, chasing money.

Then I ran into Father McMenemy, a Catholic priest I had met as a boy in Wormwood Scrubs Prison.

"Good morning, Father. Do you remember me? My name is Jimmy O'Connor." I told him where we had met. Yes, he remembered me. I asked him if he could help me, because I needed a doctor. Strangely enough, there wasn't a doctor available; no first aid, nothing, no rations. Someone was making some tea in a petrol can. I had a cup and was given a couple of aspirins to take away the pain. By this time a big lump had come up under my arm. I found a house with a French doctor; he was a miserable-looking bastard and reluctantly took me downstairs into a basement. It looked like a dungeon. He put my arm in a sling, took my temperature, gave me an injection and shrugged his shoulders without a smile or a goodbye.

My cockney pal was still with me. He didn't leave me. Sticking with me cost him his life. We wandered down the street together and smelt the aroma of coffee beans. We looked through the french window and asked the people for some coffee. They wouldn't give us any, said we were running away.

"Yeah," I said. "And don't worry. We'll come back again. He that lives and runs away, returns and comes another day."

Still they gave us nothing, so old bill came out again, out came the .45s. They worked wonders. We never used them, never fired a shot at any time. We got our coffee.

Holding my right arm, the cockney kid managed to jump the queue of thousands to get us to a small boat. Circling round the harbour were a couple of ships waiting to take us away, but it was impossible to get us all away. I was given priority because I was wounded. The kid was still with me. We passed a small hospital ship which I could have got on, and wish I had, but it would have meant leaving the cockney kid and he stuck with me, so I didn't want to lose him.

We went on a seventeen-thousand-tonner called the *Lancastria*, jammed like sardines. Six thousand troops were on board this ship; nuns were coming on board, people from the British Embassy. They were all going below. Most of the troops were on deck.

I was lucky in one way that I was ill. I went to the sick bay which consisted of four bunks. A medical orderly took my temperature. He picked up the phone to contact the ship's doctor and put me to bed, giving me a couple of tablets.

I still had my valise with the loot. They took my jacket off. I kept my trousers on. I lay on the bed and thought thank Christ for that. At least I'll wake up in England. Marseilles and Algiers were all out of the question. I'd see my wife and kid. That was my lot, the end of my war, the last time they'd see me in khaki. I was asleep in a few minutes.

At twenty past three on June 17th, 1940, three weeks after Dunkirk, I was thrown out of bed. I looked up. The door was above my head. The ship righted itself. I opened the door. Outside was a young airman.

"What's the matter, son?" I asked.

"Oh, nothing. We've just shot a Jerry down."

Pieces of fabric were coming down between the decks, but I took his word for it and got back into bed. Wallop, I was out of it again. I thought I don't know about 'shot a Jerry down'. There's something a bit dodgy here. I went out on deck. The ship was sinking. A bomb had gone straight down through the funnel and blown the bottom of the ship out. I ran into Father McMenemy, who told me the ship was sinking. He asked me to go below. There were nuns down below. I followed him. I'd lost the cockney kid. The priest tried to make it through the fire but it was impossible. He was burnt and he turned back. I remembered my father telling me how, when he was a seaman, he had jumped boat in Ceylon and the boat was sunk.

"If you're ever on a ship and it's going down, get away from it."

By this time Jerry was machine-gunning. The sea was on fire. Mugs were cutting the ropes of lifeboats, but there was one man with plenty of self-control, a petty officer called Harry Grattidge. He was calling out in non-nautical terms, "To the right of the ship, to the left of the ship," thinking that he could balance the weight. No one realised the extent of the damage at the bottom of the ship. I ran around the deck. Father McMenemy was helping the wounded and praying for people who had been machine-gunned. I looked for the cockney kid and I found him.

"Go on," I said. "Get in the sea."

"I can't swim."

"What do you mean you can't swim? Dogpaddle. Get in the sea and get away from this ship. Run round and see if you can get yourself a lifebelt."

I went into the sea. I just missed the fire. My valise in front of me, I kept pushing away, pushing away. I swam on my back. When I hit the water my right forefinger busted and I felt complete relief, not sick or ill any more. I felt better and stronger and floated on my back, pushing my valise which fortunately was made of wood. Then a dirty big wave came along and took the valise away from me. I swam towards it, but it got further away from me until eventually it was out of sight.

The sea was very rough. I saw a boat in the distance coming towards me. I swam to it, and then to my surprise she turned around and went the other way. I swam for about two hours on my back. Then I turned over to swim on my front and saw a little rubber dinghy in front of me loaded with about nine men. I swam towards it. There was a piece of rope hanging from the side and I hung on to it. They were paddling away. One of the bastards didn't even want me to hold the rope because it was overloaded. Nevertheless I did.

I was picked up by a minesweeper called the *Cambridgeshire* and then transferred to the *John Holt* of Liverpool. I was actually pulled aboard by a boxer I knew in Kilburn, a happy-go-lucky fellow. He rubbed my cheeks, massaged me, put a blanket round me and got me a cocoa tin of rice and some water. I was in the hold of the ship and within an hour or so was feeling better.

While I had been swimming on my back I heard "Roll out the barrel" being sung and thought it was a ship's radio. It wasn't. It was the men on the keel of the ship. I saw it keel over and they were singing "Roll out the barrel" as they were going to their death. They just couldn't swim. They didn't bother to get away from the boat. I thought they must be mad. In the distance they looked like gnats. It took twenty-two minutes for the ship to sink. The survivors were nine hundred out of six thousand. It was the biggest disaster of the war.

By the time we arrived in England I was feeling very perky. There were characters with their faces burnt, their bodies burnt; some were blinded, wounded. I helped them as much as I could.

I still had my body belt with the money, and took it to a petty officer's cabin. They ironed it out for me and dried it; quite a lot of money, but no one asked me where I got it from. They weren't interested. I was. I'd lost about £20,000, but at least I had something out of the war; I had my life. That was the most important thing. Some of those poor bastards were blind and couldn't see.

There wasn't anything for them to eat. When we came alongside the quay at Plymouth I ran off the ship into the railway buffet, followed by two redcaps running after me. I was bollock naked. I nicked a tray of Cornish pasties and ran back to the ship to give them out. Fuck the railway canteen, I thought.

We were marched along the quayside and given strips of blanket. Some were put in buses or ambulances. Half of Plymouth turned out; they had had the word that we were coming in. There were buses up the slope. I saw a taxi rank. He was a nice man of Devon. I went up to him.

" 'Ere, mate, do us a favour."

"What's that?"

"Do you want to earn yourself twenty-five quid?"

"What?"

"Twenty-five pounds. Drive me to London."

He looked at me and thought I was raving mad. All of a sudden, two redcaps got hold of me and I was put into a bus which took us to the naval hospital in Plymouth.

That night I slept well. In the morning I woke up, looked round the ward and saw these characters with their faces bandaged. Some had black stuff all over their faces, their arms, their legs. A young lady visitor was coming round trying to comfort us. I didn't need any comforting. In fact, I told the sister, "Sister, I'm all right. Let me get out of here." She was a toughie. She just took hold of my arm and gave it one good squeeze. All the pus shot out of it; quite a relief.

I called the visitor over to me. "Miss, do me a favour. Go out and get everybody in the ward some chocolate, newspapers and fruit. Here's some money. And while you're there, get me a pair of trousers, a pair of shoes, a jacket and a pullover. I'm going to go round the ward." She was only a young girl, about nineteen. I gave her a hundred pounds. She came back loaded. I thought it'll be away for me tonight. I waited for the sister to go off duty, change over.

The new sister wanted me to wear a blue uniform.

"Yes, sister, I'll wear that. Give it to me. I'll put it on in a minute."

In the meantime I was looking all round the place. I thought I must get to London.

Suddenly I was called into her office and told I was being transferred then and there by train to Sutton Emergency Hospital. That's handy, I thought. That suits me. Away I went on the train with other soldiers, and said goodbye to those poor bastards, some of whom are still alive today in Roehampton Hospital, blind and limbless.

When I arrived in Sutton Emergency Hospital one of the first people I saw in bed was Paddy Burn. I couldn't help laughing when I saw him. When I went up to speak to him and shake hands, he burst into tears. He'd lost all his money as well. He was on the same ship as I was and I hadn't known it.

"What are you worrying about? You've got your life," I said.

"I've been in two wars. I'm too old now. It's the only chance I'll ever get of thieving any money like that again."

They kept me in there for a few days under observation. I made out I was a nutter suffering from shellshock, talking to myself and doing all sorts of funny things. I thought, I'll get my ticket here. Someone said, "Mind how you go. You might finish up in Rampton." I thought will I?

In the afternoon my mother and father came to see me, their wounded hero son. Of course, the old man was pleased to see me, told me that he hadn't been knocking her about, and she confirmed it. And I started to unload. When he saw the money he said, "That's my boy. I guessed you'd come back with something." Then he tapped me for a tenner. When I told him what I'd lost he nearly cried. Anyway, I thanked him for the empty registered letters he'd been sending me.

The time came to say goodbye. We were having tea on the lawn. "You're joking. Goodbye! I'm coming with you."

I walked down to the gate slowly. There were a couple of soldiers on guard. "Is it all right if I just walk down to the bus to say goodbye to my mother and father?"

"Of course, son. It's only just across the road."

I nipped on to the bus and down to the station, and that was the end of my army career as far as I was concerned. But I still hadn't got my discharge, and that was what I needed badly.

When I arrived home in Kilburn and knocked at the door they were amazed to see me. My wife and son were living with her parents and had received a notice from the War Office that I had been reported missing. My wife fainted.

The first thing I went for was the presents. Father-in-law took off his braces. I had money machined inside them. I found the toys I had sent my kid, took them to pieces and out came the money. The table was loaded with money.

After a few days at home I decided I'd go and report back to the R.A.S.C. depot suffering from partial loss of memory. I went to Sutton in civilian clothes and walked into the store.

"My name is O'Connor." I didn't tell them I was acting sergeant. They asked me my rank.

"I don't know."

"Where have you come from?"

"I don't know."

"What are you doing here?"

"Well, this is where I was last time."

"What do you mean, this is where you were?"

"Well, I was on a ship and it was bombed. We went to Plymouth and I can't remember nothing since then."

"Well, where have you been?"

"I don't know where I've been."

While I was talking to them the officer who looked like David Niven went past. He looked at me.

"Sergeant," he said.

"What did you say?" I said.

"You're Sergeant James O'Connor."

"My name's James O'Connor. I'm not a sergeant. I don't think I am, anyway."

"I sent you with a convoy."

"Me, sir? I don't know what you're talking about. All I know is I was on this ship and then I was in the sea. Then I was in the hospital. Then I went to another hospital and I don't know where I've been since then, but I've been ducking and diving. I went up the pictures . . . I tell you what . . . are we going to Egypt or something to fight the Germans?"

He looked at me. He thought, I've got a right nutter here.

I was sent to Croydon under canvas. The regimental sergeant major was a well-known boxing referee who used to run a dirty low-down dive of a spieler before the war. He was as bent as arseholes, but there he was, acting like Field Marshal Montgomery. When he saw me, he knew me.

I didn't sleep in camp. I had someone straightened. They used to book me out. One night at a pub in Maida Vale I used I met two very attractive girls and bought them several drinks. I had plenty of money on me and was in civilian clothes. A couple of Canadian soldiers were trying to knock the girls off. They kept boasting how they'd travelled thousands of miles to fight for people like me. What was I doing in civilian clothes? Why wasn't I in the army? I told them to mind their own business. There was a fight outside the pub. I chinned one of them and then just ran. One of the girls was running behind me.

"Follow me." She opened the door of a house; in I went, and stayed the night with her.

When I went back to camp next morning I was placed under close arrest for being absent from an overseas draft. That draft would have saved me from conviction for a murder I did not commit. You couldn't have wished for a better post; one sergeant and twelve men—I was the sergeant—to be sent to Bermuda. I was adjudicated. I assured them it was one draft I didn't want to miss. I told them how much I wanted to go overseas.

But in the meantime the sergeant major in Kate Carney's army had shopped me and told them I was a convicted criminal. I was discharged, given my papers, and told that my services were no longer required. Now that was a beautiful licence because the coppers were always pulling people up. They used to come in and turn a pub over. You had to produce your identity card. Why aren't you in the army? People were on the run all over the place. I was free. There was my licence. I went home and showed the old man.

"There it is. You said you were going to chop my fucking arms off. I got my ticket, Dad. Now I'll show you how to get plenty of money."

He was as proud of me as if I had got my degree at Oxford.

"I've done it," I said. "It's taken me nine months. What were you moaning about?"

We both went out and got pissed.

I went back home and lived with my wife and my son. I took up my old profession of being a screwsman again, and grafted with a man called Jock the Fitter who is dead now, an ex-Borstal boy and carpenter. He could open a safe like a tin of sardines. He used to pop the rivets off the back like no one's business.

5

"Verdict Murder—By Persons Unknown"

After some successful crimes in London with Jock the Fitter, followed by a round of nightclubs, birds and drinking, I decided that we ought to go to the West Country and try and do a few jewellers' shops. I wanted to make Swindon in Wiltshire as a base for our activities and, of course, to see my country girl and my daughter. We found a way to get there, legally, and with a licence to thieve again.

A firm called Drinkwater & Company gave us a job driving two new Dodge tipping lorries to Swindon and from there we made fifteen- and twenty-mile runs with hard core to an aerodrome that was being built just outside Swindon. After finishing our day's work as lorry drivers, we returned to our flat and changed our clothes. By this time we had a couple of lock-ups for crooked cars with wrong number plates, and set out nightly on expeditions to Bristol, Gloucester, Cirencester, Taunton; the old family jeweller or the modern jeweller, we didn't care which.

One evening we arrived in Bath, parked the car at the side of the river and started looking for a pub. While we were walking along the street we passed a jeweller's shop, Messrs Leslie & Company. It had a couple of insurance paddies and two or three other locks. They were no problem to us. We robbed the jeweller's and replaced the insurance locks with our own padlocks. In actual fact, I said 'Good night' to a police constable as I was leaving the premises and locking the doors. It was March 11th, 1941.

That same night we drove from Bath to Swindon. In Commercial Road, Swindon, was a wholesale tobacconist. We decided to do this on the same night, and cleared them out of all the tobacco they had. The following day I sold the tobacco to a local J.P., a so-called pillar of respectability. Then we caught the Cheltenham Flier back to London.

That evening I went with Jock and my bird to see Izzy Farrer, a jeweller by profession and a receiver of stolen property. We went to his club in Oxford Street. The club was managed by a man called George Sewell, a man known to me as a confidence trickster and receiver of stolen jewellery or anything else stolen. George Sewell had been informed by Izzy Farrer that I had money and jewellery. He tried to con me with a story and asked me for money. I gave him a watch and chain that I knew was of little value to get rid of him and promised to see him the next day, although I had no intention of doing so. I had no time for thieves' ponces or receivers.

Jock and I disposed of the jewellery elsewhere. We shook hands and parted as friends. In March 1941 I decided to give up thieving and become a haulage contractor. I now had sufficient capital to buy a couple of lorries. I told my wife that this was the end, and went in search of my pal Bill, who was a very good mechanic. We went to look for a vehicle.

Bill and I bought a lorry and began to work in London, but Jock the Fitter had left Swindon without paying the rent to the garage proprietor. The owner became suspicious, knocked off the two padlocks and found two crooked cars inside which Jock had told me he had dumped. I had taken his word for it.

On April 9th, 1941, the police tried to arrest me for the theft of a car in Swindon. I was also wanted for breaking and entering the wholesale tobacconist in Commercial Road, Swindon.

On the evening of Easter Monday, April 14th, 1941, my father was arrested and taken to Scotland Yard as me. He was later released.

On Tuesday, April 15th, 1941, I went to my pal Bill's house. We had many things to discuss, including log books and insurance. His house was about a hundred yards from a little turning, called No. 2 Hampton Road, Kilburn. When we passed the house we saw the street was full of police. I didn't want to hang about because I knew I was wanted. I didn't stop to ask questions. The police had in actual fact just found the dead body of a man called George Alfred Ambridge.

On Friday, April 18th, 1941, I read a coroner's report in the local paper, the *Kilburn Times*: 'Verdict Murder—By Persons Unknown'.

In May 1941 I moved with my wife and son to Stockwell, South London, where I started up a business. I now had three tipping lorries and was doing quite well. I was on the run, wanted by the police, but in those days I wasn't very well known in South London, and those who did know me were not informers. But one informer, known as Bill Banner, did tell me that I was wanted for questioning in connection with the Kilburn murder.

In June 1941 the police came round calling at various houses and furnished flats in the Stockwell Road area looking for a notorious jailbreaker who had escaped from Dartmoor and reached London, a remarkable feat in those days. My wife satisfied the police, but as they were leaving she pulled the curtain to one side and aroused the suspicion of one of the coppers. He mentioned this at the police station as he was going off duty. Two of his colleagues called to have a second check up. I made out that I was not James O'Connor but Timothy O'Connor and managed to convince them that I was my brother. I looked at the window which was on the first floor, thinking I could make a dive for it. When I looked at that window one of the policemen was just leaving the room.

"Just a minute, Mr O'Connor, would you show us your right forearm?"

I knew it was all over and felt relieved.

"Don't bother, guv'nor. I'm James O'Connor." On my right forearm was tattooed "Mother" and "I love Flo". The police came down from Swindon to arrest me and took me back by train. The Wiltshire policeman told me how tough he was and even that he was carrying a gun, which amused me. I was known to be good at escaping from policemen.

I came to the conclusion that what Bill Banner had told me about being wanted for questioning in connection with a murder I knew nothing whatsoever about was nonsense, otherwise they would not have let me leave London.

When I came up in front of the Swindon Magistrates it was just like Kate Carney's police court. I couldn't believe it. The witnesses for the prosecution weren't called from outside the court. They were actually in court listening to each other's evidence. I was remanded in custody at Swindon Police Station and stayed there for two or three days. Of course, being a cockney we can be a bit of a nuisance sometimes and they got fed up with me. I tried to escape and as a result was transferred to Gloucester Prison. I didn't fancy being in the hands of the

Wiltshire police. I couldn't straighten them, but I had one in London straightened. I tried to think how I could get myself in the hands of the London police to get myself a short sentence. I contacted the copper I had straightened. He came to see me. I offered him some money if he could get me charged in London with a crime that could keep me in London, even if I had not committed it. I'd even have a chance of getting out of it if he gave evidence for me. He put his cards on the table.

"I can't help you, Ginger. The guv'nor's outside."

"The guv'nor. What's he here for?"

"The Kilburn murder. We got a statement from a man that involves you. People say that you may have hit the man too hard. A man says you flashed some jewellery to him."

I laughed. "Do you think I'm a murderer?"

"No, son, I don't, but you may have hit him a bit too hard."

"Leave off," I said. "Leave off."

Anyway, I agreed to see the guv'nor. It was my prerogative to refuse to see any policeman.

In came Charlie Ferrier, the local D.I. in my manor. As a result of the questions he asked me about the man who, he said, had been murdered on Easter Saturday, I really began to feel that I was a suspected murderer. Gawd help us, I thought, what are they trying to do to me? I never believed they'd frame a man for murder. I must say in fairness to Charlie Ferrier that he told my wife that he knew that I didn't do the murder and was satisfied that I had nothing to do with it. It was just a formality. I was a wanted man at the time and had had my hair dyed black by two girls and looked a bit like George Robey. Most of my actions had been highly suspicious. If I had been a copper I would have reacted in the same way.

About the middle of July 1941 I was transferred from Gloucester Prison to await my trial at Hampshire Assizes. I broke the eleventh commandment, never to plead guilty, just to beat the twenty-four witnesses who came by coach from Swindon to give evidence against me. I pleaded guilty to the lesser charges, which is commonly known in the legal profession as "having a deal'. This takes place between the defending counsel, the prosecutor and the judge in his chambers. The judge was Justice Charles, who was notorious for his heavy sentences and his severity.

Having pleaded guilty, counsel, who I had retained and paid, in my opinion unfortunately got all his facts mixed up. He spoke with an Oxford accent and told the tough hardened judge that his client "did not want to dilapidate in His Majesty's prisons". Well, I was fully aware of that and so was the judge. Counsel was trying to paint me whiter than white, but I knew that with this particular judge it was better for me to paint myself grey.

I asked the judge if I could dismiss this counsel and speak for myself.

"Certainly," he said.

I told him, "My Lord, I was in the British Expeditionary Force, but I wasn't no hero. The only thing I can say in my favour is that I did volunteer to go overseas with the Expeditionary Force. I was on a ship that was bombed. I have a wife. I have a child. I think crime is a mug's game. You know it's a mug's game. There is only one thing I ask you. I don't want to dilapidate in jail, but I know I'm going to. Would you make it as light as you can, sir?"

He laughed and smiled and nodded his head. Jock the Fitter had been sentenced to eighteen months at the previous assizes and he had been found not guilty to the breaking and entering. He gave me nine months. I was very happy because it was the end of the assizes and, as it had been going on for five weeks, that was taken into consideration. I thanked Justice Charles for his light sentence and went off to do my time.

But at Winchester jail I was put in the hospital wing under mental observation by Dr Christie. I learned later on that he specialised in insanity. Or maybe it was just a hobby, because I've never known a prison officer specialise in anything except Dr Grey in Grendon Hall. He's the best doctor in a prison in this country.

Being a fit person, I complained. They ignored me. I was very worried when Dr Christie began to cross-examine me about the murder of George Alfred Ambridge. It was most obvious to me that I was number one suspect and was being treated like a murderer. I wondered what they were trying to do; certify me as insane? I must admit I was a bit scared.

I became friendly with a right con man called John Halliday alias Granville Clark. He told me that it was rumoured that I was labelled as a murderer. He seemed an intelligent, educated man and I was influenced by him.

The jail was overcrowded. I was transferred to Cardiff jail and still treated as a murder suspect. From there I was transferred to Wandsworth where I sent a note to a pal of mine telling him that the police were trying to pin a murder on me and I was getting worried. There was I, in Wandsworth jail, in a hospital cell, being treated as a nutter; a fit man, A1 physically and mentally.

By this time the case had been taken over by Inspector Nat Thorp. He came to see me a couple of times in Wandsworth jail. I denied the murder which I had not committed. On the morning of January 12th, 1942, I was due for release, I went across to reception with other prisoners, got myself dressed, looked in the mirror, put on my tie. I missed my diamond tiepin and my cufflinks. The other prisoners' belongings were laid out there, and I asked for mine. I was thinking when I get out of here I'll have a drink down Covent Garden, go over the water to see a few friends and get back to business as a haulage contractor. When I asked for my tiepin and cufflinks they said, "The chief wants to see you."

I went across to see the chief, a tall, long bastard.

"Where's my tiepin?"

"I've got to inform you that Scotland Yard is at the gate to see you."

"You dirty, long bastard," I said. "You had me locked up in hospital under observation, incommunicado from the rest of the outside world, knowing full well. I know I've been suspected for a long time. I'm no fool."

I thought it couldn't be true; they wouldn't do this to me; they couldn't want to see me for that. I wondered what crime they really wanted to see me for.

Anyway, I went to the gate although I should have been released. According to law, I've never been released from that sentence. Thorp was panicking and shaking all over the place. He had a new patent type of handcuff, useful for flipping on, and he flipped them on to my wrist. Without any caution or messing about he said, "We are going to arrest you for the murder of George Ambridge."

I said it was no good him telling me he was going to arrest me for the murder of George Ambridge. He'd already done so. When I was taken out through the wicker gate, of course, I was in handcuffs. My wife was outside screaming and hooting.

I was taken to Harrow Road police station, and from there to Willesden Court for a two-minute appearance for formal remand to Brixton jail, where I shared a ward with twelve men waiting to be tried for murder.

I met a couple of dozen murderers before I left Brixton jail because I was on remand for about ten weeks. They were a motley crowd of strange people; some withdrawn, some would talk too much. There is a snobbery amongst murderers. The man who killed his wife despised the man who killed the 'Babes in the Wood'. The man who killed the 'Babes in the Wood' despised the cockney charged with murdering an old man. The cockney charged with killing the old man despised the man who murdered five prostitutes. Trevor Evans, who was awaiting trial for murdering an old lady off the Cromwell Road while she was writing him a receipt for the rent he was paying, despised everybody. He was intelligent and self-educated and first went to prison in 1913 charged with stealing one shilling from a woman's purse. For that, his first offence, he was sent to Portland jail for three years' penal servitude. This made him a very bitter man. He became a great confidence trickster and once posed as an admiral visiting and inspecting the fleet. He had done everything except one thing; he had never before used violence. He had long, beautiful nails, but by the time he had finished his remand he had eaten them down to the knuckles.

"You're a bit late, mate, with all your experience," I said, "All your years in the jail. Why didn't you try and make out you were insane?"

"I left it too late," he said. He was nearing sixty-five years of age.

"I shouldn't think they'd hang you at your age," I said. Just the mention of the word 'hanging' used to make everybody sick, but I was trying to cheer the fellow up. Basically I love a bit of humour. I used to be a happy fellow, full of fun. Anyway, they hanged him despite his age.

Gordon Cummings was a young supercilious Air Force officer. He said his father was a schoolmaster at Eton, and was absolutely convinced that being an educated person he was a different breed to us illiterate bastards and would therefore not be hanged. He killed about five prostitutes, cut them to pieces and stuffed various objects up their pussies.

We used to walk round on exercise with each other and I liked having someone different to talk to every day. I was always interested in people and how they ticked.

One right nutter there had killed three people because they refused him membership of the Chiswick Tennis Club. Every time the governor came in I used to get him at it. I said, "Now look here, they're keeping you in this prison for nothing. You've done nothing wrong. You just go and tell that governor you've got to meet Winston Churchill. You've got a special assignment. You're going to the Middle East and your real name is Colonel Vadistock. Give him the code number, M.I.21. Tell him to have a car here at four o'clock and you're taking me with you. I've come into this prison especially to select people for the Secret Service. I have chosen you and I am promoting you to colonel."

Every day this guy drove the governor mad. He couldn't stand it. He sent for me at the finish.

"Connor," he said, "turn it up."

"Turn what up, Governor?"

"Don't keep driving me mad and sending that character along to me."

"You've got to laugh, have something to pass the time away," I said. "He's happy. He doesn't even know he's killed anybody, if he has killed anybody."

Anyway, he went off to trial. He was back the same day to Brixton in civilian clothes.

I asked him how he got on. He started to pack his kit and take his personal possessions from his locker.

"How did you get on?"

"Oh," he said, "I'm going home."

"What do you mean, going home?"

"Oh," he said, "they said I wasn't fit to plead."

"You've had a right result," I said, but I thought to myself you're going home all right. He was on his way to Broadmoor. I suppose the poor bastard is still there.

A miserable bastard of a screw was in charge of us, another war dodger. As far as he was concerned, we were all murderers. He had found us guilty before we ever had our trial. It was freezing cold, snowing, but he wouldn't let us light a fire until six o'clock. I used to light it during the day and as fast as he outed it I lit it. What could they do to me? Nothing. I just used to tell them to fuck off.

One little guy there never spoke to anybody the whole ten

weeks. He spent all his time reading Westerns. I asked about him later and they told me he was reading a Western right up to the time they took him to the scaffold.

The most cheerful one of the lot was Mack, the Canadian soldier. We were very happy when we heard he was found not guilty. From the head of the table he used to scream out, "Rob the hangman", and used to torture a few of the people sitting there who had consciences, "Guilty or not guilty?" He made cracks about Pierrepoint, the hangman.

"When he comes in there, before he grabs hold of you he hits you over the head with a hot sock full of shit, kicks you up the bollocks, someone pulls a lever, drops you down the hole, and two of them swing on your feet singing, 'Here we go round the mulberry bush, the mulberry bush . . .' " Mack had a deep laugh and looked a little like Ernest Borgnine, the actor.

Instead of bogging you down with all the details of the witnesses for the prosecution, I'll give you a breakdown of the events leading to my trial.

During the Easter weekend in 1941, between 12th and 15th April, George Alfred Ambridge of Hampton Road, Kilburn, was murdered. There was no immediate arrest. On the night of the murder I was in Kilburn with my wife at a party. During the following months a number of men, mostly from the Kilburn area, were suspected and questioned by the police. They included Henry Waterton, a man with criminal convictions, later a witness for the prosecution; George Sewell, a man with criminal convictions, later a witness for the prosecution; Frederick Andrews, who was accused by George Sewell, and I have Sewell's statement about this, obtained after twenty-seven years; Les Allen, accused by Henry William Waterton; Bill, my friend, tried and quite rightly acquitted; and myself, James O'Connor, tried and convicted for a murder I did not commit.

None of these men named had anything whatsoever to do with the murder of George Alfred Ambridge, and to the best of my knowledge none of them even knew him. Neither Bill nor I called witnesses or gave evidence for the defence. I saw my counsel, Hector Hughes, Q.C., Member of Parliament for Aberdeen, for the first time on the morning of the trial.

The principal witness for the prosecution was George Sewell, a receiver and police informer who had also been questioned by the police in connection with the same murder. He made a statement leading the police to believe that I had been involved in a murder and the watch I had given him was part of the proceeds of the crime. This was the watch from the jewellery shop in Bath, and I had in fact given it to him well before the murder, as I will later establish.

I was considered to be unlucky in my judges; Groome Johnson at my trial and Lord Caldecott at the appeal. Neither was famous for his impartiality or sympathy towards a man in the dock. It appeared to anybody listening, even a layman, that the principal prosecutor was the judge himself. There was no doubt that Groome Johnson and my counsel, Hector Hughes, had an old vendetta.

My counsel was shot down. The jury's verdict was "We find William ——— not guilty of murder, my Lord. We find James O'Connor guilty of murder."

I looked at Bill. He was in a daze. He turned round two or three times in the dock.

"Let William ——— be released from the dock," said Mr Justice Groome Johnson. Bill couldn't get out quick enough. He couldn't even find the door. He was innocent and the jury found him innocent. He looked at me and left the dock.

I was a fatalist. I knew they were going to find me guilty. The Clerk of the Court was speaking a sentence that had been repeated many times at the Old Bailey for people convicted of murder, innocent or guilty. "Have you anything to say before sentence is passed upon you?"

"Yes," I said, "I've got something to say." I noticed my solicitor was sweating. He thought I was going to have an outburst of temper. I told the judge, "I have not had a fair trial. You have been vindictive to me throughout this trial. The jury have only found me guilty because you directed them to. I am not afraid to die, but I do not want to die for a murder I did not commit."

Whip-It-Quick, the master criminal, his Clerk quickly put the black hat upon the head of the judge. He looked like Will Hay. It was a comedy. It nearly fell over his eyes as he went to sentence me to death. But I didn't want to listen to all that old cobblers about your body will be taken from here to there and from whence you came. I turned quickly to descend the stairs and took a cigarette from my pocket and lit it, but the screws remonstrated with me and pulled me round facing the judge, enabling him to see the cigarette. The journalists called me 'Cigarette Killer' when they wrote their headlines. When I lost my appeal, the press said, 'Cigarette killer to die'. That is journalism for you.

When I descended the stairs of No. 1 Court there were half a dozen screws waiting for me. I must confess my knees were a bit shaky by the time I reached the bottom. I went into one of the cells. A couple of Jewish men from Manchester whom I didn't know were up on a black market thing. They sent me a couple of hundred cigarettes. Dr Grierson opened the door, came in and ironically enough said, "Would you like a cigarette?" He was only nobbling me because I had smoked in the dock. Two screws were locked in the cell with me.

Outside the side door of the Old Bailey a crowd of people assembled, friends and morbid nosey parkers, to gaze at a man just sentenced to death, hoping to see something, expecting him to look other than human. I was still human. I wasn't even a murderer. I didn't have a gun in each hand or a stiletto in my mouth. Someone waved and shouted out, "Goodbye, good luck, Ginger," as I got into the car and left for Pentonville.

We stopped at the traffic lights at the Caledonian Road. A car pulled up alongside, some crooked friends, a racing mob known as the Whites. They had come back from the races. They were the guv'nors at the point-to-points and were on their way to start the night's drinking. The jailers felt uneasy. The mob in the other car got excited and called out, "Keep your chin up, boy." Our driver, as the lights changed to green, soon pulled away. I began to think fast and hard, then remembered my handcuffs. I felt choked.

6

I was to be hanged in the suit I was convicted in

I was taken to the condemned cell at Pentonville. The Brixton jailers had to deliver me to the Pentonville jailers and get a receipt for my body. I heard one of the Pentonville screws say, "I've heard about this bastard." I knew then that someone had been at the mix and told them that I was a bit of a nuisance. Make no mistake about it, this poor old boy who had been murdered, and there had been no doubt according to the evidence of Sir Bernard Spilsbury, had had his head smashed in, blood and brains were spattered all over the wall, and some people are not disposed to look too kindly towards a person who they believe has done that. But all that was really wrong with me was that at twenty-three I was anti-social, not amenable to discipline. I was not servile and spoke straight and told a person what I thought of him, good or bad, and I shocked people by my frankness. There was one thing I wasn't. I was not a murderer, but to these people I was a murderer. I had no conventional habits. I was a complete egoist and individualist, emotional and with a sharp tongue. I never tried to make people like me. But this whore's son who'd never met me before had to call me a bastard. I looked at the speaker, then at the principal officer in charge.

"Guv'nor," I said, "to save yourself a lot of trouble, don't ever let that screw in this cell while I'm here."

Screw, as you know by this time, is the name given to jailers by the prisoners. To them they're all screws, turnkeys, jailers, counting your bodies every night. I must say in fairness to the principal screw, he ordered him out. He went. I wasn't in a good mood waiting to be hanged.

All that the other screws were concerned with was checking my personal clothing. I was to be hanged in the suit I was dressed in when convicted. I took it off and laid it on the bed. Lying there were two prison uniforms, not ordinary prison garb but condemned cell clothing, with no buttons and the trouser flies fastened with tapes. The shapeless coats and trousers were made of grey cloth. There were two collar-attached cotton shirts with black stripes, two pairs of black socks, and some carpet slippers. I could have shoes, but I wasn't going any place. The tapes made me grin. They wanted to make sure I was alive when I went to the scaffold, even if they had to carry me there. If I resisted I would be grabbed by the arms, pinioned to a bed-board and put on the trap like that, trussed up like a chicken. The main object once you're in the death cells is to see you don't cheat death. Amory, the wartime traitor, was in the last stages of TB and dying when Pierrepoint hanged him.

I picked up one of the suits. It bore the surname of Bill, who had been tried and acquitted. I threw it off the bed.

"You can take that. He won't need it now. He's very likely in bed with his old woman."

In 1942 Pentonville was exactly one hundred years old. Half of a wing was taken up with the condemned cell, two cells knocked into one, where the prisoner lives. There were two doors through which to enter, a door on the left leading to the toilet, and a hidden door on your right, flush with the wall, painted over, which led into the execution shed. I was not aware of that door, it was so cleverly painted.

I didn't sleep my first night in the condemned cell. The screws came in and changed my clothes at ten o'clock when they changed shifts. I had some right miserable bastards in there with me. At least if you're on your way to your death it would have been nice to have someone who can make you laugh.

I had one bit of luck, a character called Fred, a good screw, but the others as usual were war dodgers. Fred was an old timer, a regular, simpatico. He hated the Condemned Cell Duty. It was the first time he had been on it in his life.

At 7 p.m. I had my first meal. You've heard all that cobblers about the luxuries the condemned cell man got. I got a pint of cocoa in a thick china mug, eight ounces of bread and half an ounce of butter. That's all, and that had to last me till breakfast. After I got the meal down I began to pace the cell. I wouldn't go to bed. I couldn't sleep. All I wanted to do was to walk up and down like Felix and think and think and think.

Six jailers were detailed to be with me. Three were on their way up from Exeter jail, detailed to stand by me in case I gave them a rough time, but what could I do? They couldn't hurt me. At ten o'clock at night the relief man arrived. I started to take off my clothes and changed into another set. The relief watch receives your body and a set of clothes that has been thoroughly searched. I didn't want to take off my clothes. I could see no sense in it. After an argument I agreed, and they gave me a pint of beer. As I drank it I could hear the boys singing over at the pub facing the Ville, Vera Lynn's song, "We'll meet again". I thought, "Oh, Christ, I hope we do, mate," but it didn't make my pint go down any easier.

Fred Parsons was a decent screw. He was obviously sorry for me. He begged me to sit down and take it easy. He suggested I might like to pass the night telling my life story. I was in no mood for reminiscences. I wanted to ask him what it felt like to be hanged, whether it was as quick as they claimed, what kind of rope they used, but all Fred would say was, "You're a long way from being dead yet, Jim." He tried to get me to play draughts or ludo. Ludo for a man waiting to be topped!

The night dragged through. I took no account of time. I knew it was morning when they brought my breakfast in, a pint of porridge, six ounces of bread and a pint of tea. For the next few hours the cell was never empty. I had visits from the governor, the prison chaplain and the Catholic priest, Father Williams, who is still alive and is now Canon Williams in Hammersmith. All of them, except the Catholic priest, didn't seem to think I was taking their calls in the right spirit. The governor asked me if I wanted anything.

"Yes," I said. "A fuck."

I was also entitled to see my father a few yards from the death cell in the visiting box. I sat one side of the window, my father on the other. There were a couple of screws with me. My father was so overcome he couldn't speak. I knew I was looking at a dying man. He had tuberculosis. He got out a few words about my mother. My eyes were full of tears and my throat seemed paralysed. I couldn't answer him. The appearance of the principal jailer cut short an embarrassing scene. He told me that the Senior Medical Officer from Wormwood Scrubs wanted to see me. The reason he came was because Pentonville Prison was actually closed. I was the only prisoner, except for two cleaners, in the prison.

This doctor had a bad reputation. His name was Dr Murdoch. He hated the underworld and put people on a water diet when they complained of tummy troubles. Having heard all about him, I looked at him. He started off, "Connor."

"O'Connor," I said. "Leave the handle on."

"If you behave yourself I'll give you cheese, jam, milk, a pint of beer a day and ten cigarettes."

I told him I was behaving myself. "But I don't want any favours from you. I just want justice." I told him he could stick his extra cheese up his arse. "Just give me what I am entitled to, nothing more, nothing less. Now my father's more important and he's waiting for me. He's more important than the jam."

I went back to the visiting box, said goodbye to my father and returned to the death cell.

The governor had to visit me every day. He came over from the Scrubs. His name was Ball, a miserable bastard, afraid to die, I should think. He always carried his little gas mask over his shoulder. I used to rib him every day when he asked me did I want anything. Of course I wanted something.

"Would you ask Pierrepoint, the hangman," I said, "if he'd do me a favour and get a rubber rope. I've got a bit of a sensitive neck." That didn't go down too well with him.

Lunch was greasy soup and potatoes. The principal officer was a very efficient screw but the worst cook in the nick, and the prison kitchen was closed. In the afternoon I had an hour's exercise and walked up and down the small concrete yard between the condemned cell and the reception building. The high prison wall was supposed to hide me from people who lived in the flats opposite the jail. It didn't. I became one of the neighbourhood sights. Sometimes I'd catch little kids staring down from the flat windows. I used to wonder if any of them would end up like me.

After exercise my wife and my mother often visited me. We'd sit and look at each other through the glass of the visiting box. The principal officer stayed with them all the time and two screws were guarding me. On one occasion five or six of my wife's relations were there. They could only talk to me in pairs and I heard one say to another, "Oh, no, you can't claim insurance money for a man who's hung." I thought what a nice lot of bastards to be related to.

Fred Parsons was there. "Fred," I said, "do me a favour. Take me back to the condemned cell." I got up. I was choked. I never even said goodbye to my wife or anybody.

He hadn't heard any of this. "What's the matter, Jimmy?" he asked.

"Take me back, Fred," I said. So Fred took me back to the condemned cell. I started to play chess with old Fred until we were too tired to move the pieces.

At times the days and nights dragged. The only breaks in the monotony were the changes in the death watch and the visits from the governor and his staff. Fred was the only screw I really talked to. The others liked to get you chatting and hoped to trap you into admitting your guilt. Anything you said went down in the Daily Occurrence Book. If you said something that could be twisted into a confession it made the authorities feel better about hanging you.

The only thing that kept me going in the condemned cell was my upbringing as a Catholic child. I was very happy to get a letter from my schoolteacher, Miss Clancy, enclosing a picture of the Sacred Heart on which she had written a prayer which she composed herself.

'Dear God, thou seest all, thou knowest all, thou canst all. I place all my faith in thee.' I still have that today. In the letter she asked me whether I would agree to see a Canon from the diocese where my school was. I did not know him, but he came to see me with Father Williams. His main concern was that he wanted to come to the scaffold with me on the day I was executed. He was very guarded in the way he put it to me. Of course, the rule was that only one priest could come with me, and I told him I would let him know, although I had already made up my mind. Having been with Father Williams for a few weeks, I wanted him to come with me to the scaffold. I was quite happy to die with him at the side of me—not on the trap, of course.

I then went to confession with Father Williams. It must have taken a couple of hours, the amount of villainy I had done in my life, but he helped me out of trouble. I told him I hadn't been confirmed. This had to be put right. I was visited by Bishop Matthew, brother of the Public Prosecutor Matthew, and a great man. He became Archbishop and a Papal Emissary to Ethiopia.

Part of Pentonville jail had been bombed to pieces by the Germans and the Bishop's red gown was flowing amongst the dust as I walked behind him to the roofless Catholic chapel where he confirmed me. My godfather was a screw called Johnson.

After forty days in the condemned cell my appeal was heard on the 4th May 1942. On the bench were Lord Chief Justice Caldecott, Mr Justice Humphreys and Mr Justice Cassels. Before the case had been going long my spirits began to rise. Mr Justice Humphreys wasn't satisfied with some of the evidence of the witnesses for the prosecution. A screw nudged me with his elbow. He said, "You're out of this, son." I thought, yeah, I'm out of it when I'm out of it. The irony of it was that but for an accident Mr Justice Humphreys would have been the judge at my trial. If he had been, I'm sure I would have been acquitted.

I have only had one shock in my life. I don't consider being bombed on the *Lancastria* was a shock. I don't consider being sentenced to death at the Old Bailey for a murder I didn't commit was a shock, but what was a shock was losing my appeal. I knew then that death was inevitable.

It wasn't even a shock on the Tuesday following the loss of my appeal when the governor came to the condemned cell. He seemed a bit upset. He didn't know how to begin, what to say. I felt sorry for him, so I helped him out.

"All right, guv," I said, "don't tell me. I know what you're going to say. The execution has been fixed for the 20th May, my birthday." It was a guess, but it was right. The governor swallowed something in his throat and nodded miserably. I think he felt worse about it than I did. I felt sorry for him in actual fact. I grinned, "That's a fucking nice birthday present."

Three extra screws were added to the death watch. They expected a change in me. After all, I hadn't been the bad lad I was supposed to have been. I must have been painted much blacker during my life than I really am.

The first person to visit me was Dr Murdoch in his Harris tweed sporting suit. They gave me my lunch at half past four: peas, carrots and some potatoes, baked and dry. He just looked in, "All right," and wanted to walk away.

"Just a minute," I said. "Just a minute." I took the cover from the plate of food and held it up. "How would you like to eat this for lunch?" He stuck his nose in to smell it and I sploshed it all down his Harris tweed suit. He wasn't too pleased with that.

When I woke up the following morning one of the new screws was puffing away at a pipe, wearing his carpet slippers. He kept farting all over the place; another war dodger. I told him to out his pipe. "This is my home. I live in it, not you. Fuck off out of the cell." I couldn't breathe. It was like a London smog. They brought my breakfast in, a can of porridge, just like concrete. Up to then the screws had been quite liberal, giving me two or three pints of milk a day. We made tea all day long, the screws and I, and drank it together. But they changed the principal officer and he stuck to the book, one pint and one pint only.

"Go and get some milk for me, boys," I said. "It's like concrete." They sent for the principal officer, a very smart man with creased trousers and his silver-grey hair brushed back smartly, tall, elegant.

"What's all the trouble?" he asked. It was the first time I'd met him.

"What's all the trouble? Look at this."

"What's wrong with it?"

"Well, you fucking well eat it," and I stuck it over his nut.

It was very embarrassing in the condemned cell. Going to the lavatory the screws watched you, have a bath and they were standing beside you. Asleep your hands had to be above the sheets, not to stop you masturbating but in case you slit your wrists and defeated the hangman.

I wrote a petition to the Secretary of State saying I was writing for my life. I wanted to inform the Home Secretary that the evidence given by George Sewell who said that I had come to his house the morning after the murder and given him a watch and chain was false; that I had, in fact, broken into and entered a jeweller's shop in Bath city and stolen a quantity of jewellery amongst which was the watch and chain I had given to George Sewell. I still have that petition which I wrote on 6th May 1942 and in which I confessed where the watch and chain had really come from.

Jock was still doing eighteen months. I wondered why he hadn't come forward and spoken the truth, but I didn't want to get him nicked. However, as a result of this statement Jock was visited by Superintendent Nat Thorp. I was later told that he would neither confirm nor deny that we ever committed a robbery in the city of Bath, but he crashed during a police chase while he was doing some villainy and died from the injuries. He died as he had lived, a thief like myself from the age of ten. He did nothing to save my life or clear my name and, like a lot of other people, he knew I was not guilty of murdering George Ambridge.

One day I had a visit from a very smart looking gentleman in a nice grey lounge suit and a homburg hat. He came to my cell and sat on the bed, stinking of whisky.

"Who the fucking hell are you?" I asked.

"Me, laddie? I'm the Prison Commissioner."

"You look drunk to me. You smell of whisky. What's your name, guv'nor?"

"My name is Alexander Patterson." The late Sir Alexander Patterson was a good man. "Laddie," he said, "I must tell you. I couldn't come into this cell to visit you unless I had one or two large scotches."

We were alone in the cell. He wasn't afraid. He sent everybody out. I thought I had better sound him out and find out what my chances are.

"Tell me, they're going to top me next week or the week after, I think. Do you think I've got any chances with the Home Secretary?" I told him the watch and chain story. He listened to me.

"Laddie," he said, "you're worth twelve dead 'uns. Anything I can do for you?"

"Yes, get rid of those two miserable bastards from Exeter. They keep talking about their increments and allowances and they're worried about the war damage done to their draper's shop. Send me a couple of screws across, a couple of youngsters, ex-service men. They are used to men. Not war dodgers like I've got."

"Your request is granted." He sent the war dodgers back to Exeter. At night time two youngsters came over from Wandsworth. They were specially selected and put themselves out to cheer me up. They didn't care whether I was innocent or guilty. That wasn't their business.

I had two days to go before my execution. It was a strange

thing, but I began to feel physically cold. I sat down with my back to the radiator. I decided I didn't want to see anybody. I didn't want to see my wife or my mother, but I felt I'd just like to see my father because I knew he was dying. Seeing my wife or my mother would upset me too much. My father came to visit me on his own in the afternoon. Then the door was pushed open and the deputy governor put his head round the door. He just smiled. I was sitting on the floor, back to the radiator, in actual fact next to the door that had been painted over and which led into the execution shed. I didn't know it. A right mug I must have looked.

He said, "Well it's come, my boy."

Being a perverse bastard, I said, "What's come?" I knew. "Come in," I said. "Don't be afraid, sticking your head round. Come in."

He had a vellum parchment which he unrolled. "His Majesty has graciously granted you a respite."

"A respite. What does that mean? Penal servitude for life?"

"I suppose so."

"What do you mean, you suppose so? It doesn't say nothing here. It just says I'm granted a respite."

They sprung the lock of the door as soon as I was reprieved. Fred was on duty. Tears came into his eyes. He was relieved and happy.

I had a quick visit from my father and he broke down. Within an hour I had changed back into my civvy clothes and was on my way in a covered wagon to Wandsworth jail.

George Harrison, an ex-screwsman who was released from Dartmoor in 1927, was a friend of my father's and had known me as a child. He came to visit me and I discovered then that the wicked bastards had kept me in the condemned cell an extra night. As a result of a petition he had sent to the Home Office, he had had a telegram from them the previous evening telling him I was reprieved. He showed it to me. The reason for the delay was that the governor could not stay the execution until he had an official document in his hands.

7

"A lifer"

I was to spend the first month of my sentence in Wandsworth, and after that was to go to a penal colony for a period at which I could only guess, ten, fifteen or even twenty years. I didn't know. I had been in the condemned cell for just on eight weeks. Now I was leaving alive.

As we drove away I found myself whistling for the first lap of the journey. Then I started to laugh. One of the screws asked me what I was laughing at. I told him about the ruse a couple of the screws had been trying to get up all week. They had a pair of scales outside the condemned cell and one of them told me that he had a bet with the other that I weighed twelve stone. The other one said I weighed about ten stone. They bet each other a packet of cigarettes. "You must be joking," I said. They were trying to get me on the scales for the hangman's drop.

At Wandsworth jail they lost no time in getting me to a cell. The custom for years had been for a reprieved man to go to hospital for observation. Nine times out of ten he lost weight in the condemned cell. I was taken to the ordinary part of the prison. When the door closed behind me, my nerves weren't too good. It was the first night I was to spend alone as a lifer. Without death watch screws the cell seemed empty, and to cheer myself up I lit a cigarette I'd saved. I'd forgotten that ordinary prisoners were not allowed to smoke until they'd reached a certain stage. The door burst open and in marched three screws led by the principal officer, who was an Irishman. We were old enemies. He told me to throw my cigarette away. I told him to get fucked and to leave me in peace. I didn't care about him or a thousand screws. I said if he didn't like it he could go and get the strong cell ready. They did.

Despite the fact that I had lost two stone, an Irish doctor, a Catholic, one of my own, passed me fit for bread and water.

I spent a lousy night and dreamed I was being hanged. Over thirty years later I still break out in a sweat when I have this nightmare.

I rang my bell, but no one answered. I kept on ringing, no answer. I picked up my chair and had a smash-up; I smashed out all the windows, broke up all the furniture. The prison was in an uproar. I heard the screws outside my door. They waited until I had quietened down. I wore myself out having the smash-up. There were only four walls and myself. I had no chance.

A single jailer gave me the personal touch. "What's the matter, Jimmy boy?"

"I've been ringing this fucking bell for half an hour. You lot of bastards wouldn't care if I was dying." He continued to kid me.

"Well," he said, "you're lucky. Your wife's at the gate, come to visit you."

This really quietened me down. I had wedged my door with the bed, the table and various objects. I took the wedge away and stood the three-card trick. As I stepped across the threshold the screws pounced on me. I grabbed the railings. Their coshes went across my knuckles. My feet didn't touch the ground. They frogmarched me down to the punishment block and dumped me in a strong cell. A strong cell has two doors. The floor is concrete. There's no table or chair and the bed is a board set in concrete. Bedding is not put in until eight o'clock at night. The diet is bread and water. The punishment block can break a man's spirit pretty quickly. I was determined they weren't going to break mine.

Finally I was reported to the governor for repeated breaches of discipline. Within a few days of being reprieved I was on my way to Dartmoor.

I was now twenty-four years of age and the first man to begin a life sentence on the Moor for fifteen years. They'd all been going to Parkhurst. Another liberty was being taken with me.

From the peak of Hessary Tor you looked down on the grey prison buildings. The mist and the low clouds opened up to show me my new home for life. I felt just about as low as a man can get. The reception wing at Dartmoor also houses the punishment cells.

Throughout the wing, silence is the rule. I found this out

from my first Dartmoor convict. Joe Kinsella was serving ten years for blackmail and although he was young when he was convicted, his hair was now snow-white. He lived alone in the punishment cells and was the orderly. The first time I saw him I spoke to him. He silenced me with a finger across his lips. I couldn't understand it. I hadn't heard any judge tell me that I couldn't talk. I went into my cell. Joe came and whispered at the door. He said that he had read my sentence on the door card and that he wanted to offer me sympathy. I felt I was talking to some Oxford don instead of an old lag. He apologised for his previous silence.

"If you're caught talking you're at once placed on report. That means you lose seven days' remission and have bread and water."

I was taken before the governor, which is normal routine on reception. He just sneered at me.

"So you're the tough guy from London, are you? Well, we're mighty tough in the West, you know, as you will find out."

I found out the hard way. I was up and down the punishment cells like a yoyo. When we were adjudicated before the governor we were unlocked one at a time at the double behind the steel bars of a cage to protect the governor from being attacked by a prisoner. When we came out we ran the gauntlet, walking down the stairs to the punishment cells, the chokie, dirty damp cells below earth level with condensation pouring down the walls. They used to throw us down, but I used to leap down and laugh, and rush into my cell quickly, turning my back against the wall. The two skinny-thin, hungry Welshmen who kicked the prisoners into their cells with their big thick boots used to laugh at me. They never touched me because I let it be known that I was going to die, but if I did someone was coming with me, either a screw or the governor. In view of my conviction this had a psychological effect on them.

In those days we were nicked for anything; having a blanket round our shoulders if we were cold, failing to complete our cell task after a day's work by gaslight, sewing mailbags eight stitches to the inch. If it was seven it was thrown back at us and we were put on punishment. I refused and decided I was never going to sew a mailbag, so I had to pay the price, down the chokie, bread and water. Down there I got more mailbags, and if I failed to complete them I was punished again. We couldn't win. They were determined to break everybody and they hated cockneys. Men were beaten up. Another bunch of war dodgers joined His Majesty's Prison Service to avoid being in His Majesty's Armed Services and at war overseas. They used to do anything to justify and hold their jobs.

I went in front of the governor for using obscene language to one of his officers. How they can give themselves that title I don't know. Half of them came out of the Home and Colonial Stores or Peak Frean's biscuits. Their standard of education was lower than mine. One screw couldn't even read or write. Only about four and a half feet tall, he was the terror of the jail. They used to call him 'Ten a day'. He used to come round with the Gestapo or the heavy mob and nick at least ten prisoners every day.

The governor generally asked you if you have anything to say before he passed punishment upon you. One day I gave this governor a bit of a shock.

"Yes, I've got something to say. I've decided I don't want to live on this earth under these circumstances, so I'm going to die." He wished me luck.

"Good," he said. "Make a good job of it."

"I will. A very good job of it. I'm going to be hanged. I'm going to kill you." He went silent for a second. "Oh, yes, we're both going to die. We'll go together. After all, you told me you were mighty tough in the West."

They lost no time. I was whipped over to the hospital for observation. I played the part as a nutter and thought I'd work my ticket to Broadmoor: anything would be better than this. I used to wash my food and say I was being poisoned, that I was Napoleon. I fed imaginary ducks drawn in chalk on the courtyard and never shaved. All my hair got matted; I didn't wash, which is the price you have to pay when playing this part. It was very difficult to keep it up. After three months I'd just about had enough. The doctor sent for me.

"O'Connor, sit down there." It was about five minutes before lunch, which consisted of rice pudding. "The magistrates are coming this afternoon." In those days just the doctor and two visiting magistrates could certify you as insane and send you to Broadmoor or Rampton. Convicted murderers, guilty or innocent, were always sent to Broadmoor. "You want to go to Broadmoor," he said.

"Who? Me? No. Me, why should I want to? I'm as sane as you are. Why should I go to Broadmoor?"

"Well," said the doctor, "I want to tell you something. With your conviction and your behaviour the last three months it's no problem for me. This afternoon two magistrates will be here at three o'clock. I can put you before them and certify you and you can go to Broadmoor."

"Well, that's very nice of you, but I don't want to go to Broadmoor."

"But you threatened to murder the governor."

"Who? Me? I never. You must be joking."

"Now listen to me, O'Connor. Go away and eat your rice pudding and think on this while you're eating it. I can send you to Broadmoor, but once you arrive there, with your conviction for murder, you will never ever get out. Now think about that."

I left him. I returned to the hospital cell which was nearly always empty. People were afraid to report sick. It was so grim there and it was also below ground level. I looked out and saw the grey walls and the grey sky and the low clouds of the moor. It's sixteen hundred feet above sea level, damp, dirty. It took me two minutes to think about it and eat my rice pudding. At two o'clock the bell went and I returned to the doctor.

"Well, O'Connor, you tell me. Sane or insane?"

"I'll settle for sanity."

"No more ducks to feed?"

"No more ducks to feed."

"No more meat to wash?"

"No more meat to wash."

"Go and get yourself a hot bath and get back to work."

I had lost a bit of weight. They put me on No. 15 party which went outside under the gun. Our guards carried guns in those days of my conviction. We were reclaiming land just outside the American cemetery, blocks weighing between twenty and twenty-five tons. We had to pummel them with a steel spar, split them with steel wedges and smash away at them with a sledge hammer until the grain was split, and then break them up smaller and smaller. The amount of food in a young man was insufficient. Our stomachs used to gnaw. We ate turnips; we had no time to wash them, but clean dirt never hurt anybody. If we were caught eating one we were nicked again. In those days we got our loaves of bread in the morning and they were supposed to last us all day long. Three times a week we were given some horrible stinking deep-freeze rotten fish with watery potatoes full of eyes, a right load of rubbish.

About this time the Prison Commissioners decided to send a couple of hundred prisoners from Parkhurst jail to Dartmoor. Among them were a dozen lifers. Quite a few of them interested me.

One lifer was Billy Birkitt. The Attorney General told the House of Commons in 1948 that there was no such thing in this country as 'natural life', no such sentence in British jurisprudence. When I repeated this information to little old Billy Birkitt, he wasn't amused, for Billy knew the only way he'd ever leave prison was feet first. He was probably the only man in England who had been three times acquitted of murder but convicted for manslaughter. Each time his victim was a married woman living apart from her husband. Even in his sixties, tough Billy Birkitt, a fisherman from Hull, was feared by the long-term prisoners. Yet he used to be old Uncle Bill to the children in Hull's trawler community, normally a likeable companion, fond of children and good company. But he had an uncontrollable temper and in a bad mood was liable to kill or injure anybody opposing him. He was one of the best men in the dangerous Iceland fishing trade. Every skipper was glad to get him as one of the crew, but when something upset him he became a demon, feared by skippers and shipmates. Billy's arms were heavily tattooed. Two tombstones figured prominently in the designs. In 1910 he joined the Navy and served in minesweepers. Then he was charged with stabbing a woman to death in Hull and found not guilty of murder but guilty of manslaughter. After twelve years' penal servitude he was released on licence, a ticket of leave as you might say. He killed another woman, stabbing her in the neck in her home in Hull. This time Birkitt was discovered unconscious from gas poisoning. Again he appeared at York Assizes. Again he was found guilty of manslaughter after being charged with murder, and this time he received ten years. After he left Dartmoor he strangled another woman in Neptune Street, Hull, and then sent a little girl for a hundred aspirins. He got himself another five hundred, mixed the lot into a paste, swallowed it and then threw himself into the River Humber. A passer-by rescued him and copped five shillings for saving him. Billy always used to complain about him. He was arrested and tried at Leeds Assizes. Again the jury found him not guilty of murder but guilty of manslaughter. Sentencing Birkitt, the judge said, "The jury have taken a merciful view of your crime. They did not know what you know and what I know. They were not allowed to know that this was the third time you have stood in the dock on a charge of murder. Each time it's been the murder of a woman with whom you've been living. Each time the jury has taken a merciful view. You've been out from your last sentence only a short while. In just over three years circumstances arise in which you are charged with the same result. I can see in your case not one redeeming feature. The sentence I pass upon you is that you be kept in penal servitude for the rest of your natural life, and when I say natural life I mean natural life."

After the Attorney General's speech in the House, Billy appealed against his sentence. The appeal was rejected.

Bill was more like a prison officer than an old lag. He never hesitated to grass and tell tales, and was responsible for many men being put in the punishment cells. He suffered from institutional rot, prison rot, a disease not in the book.

The number of men in from the North of England for killing whores staggered me. Little Steve from Newcastle killed a girl in his home town and also confessed to the killing of French Fifi in Soho. He had a result. He got sixteen years. Steve was a hard little case when he started his sentence and lost a lot of remission.

Geordie was another serving a fourteen stretch. After killing a prostitute he had walked into a police station and confessed. The coppers laughed and charged him with being drunk, but in the morning when the body was found by a milkman they altered the charge to murder. Geordie spent his time in jail studying history.

The most pathetic little character was Robbie. He told me he had killed his wife's lover. A quiet little man, he wouldn't have said boo to a goose. Robbie used to call at the local on Saturdays at noon for a quick beer. One day a pal of his said, "If you go home now you'll discover something." Robbie went home. The sequel was the death sentence followed by a reprieve and life.

Having listened to many of these murderers, blackmailers and rapists, I began to think about drama and decided I would like to become a dramatist. I asked the deputy governor, who was a bit sorry for me because I think he knew I was innocent, if he could help. I did a course of drama with Ruskin College, Oxford. They were very pleased with my work and asked the Home Office for permission for me to continue the correspondence course during the summer break. My unseen tutor at Oxford used to send me titles—The Rehearsal, The Sea—and I wrote thirty-minute plays to fit the subject. Then he told me that my plays were too violent. I wrote back and said what about the Greek tragedies. I also explained that I lived amongst violence in a very violent world. He told me that if I continued in this vein I had no hopes whatsoever. The tutor was wrong. *Three Clear Sundays*, a play I wrote for television, has been shown nearly all round the world. Some newspapers said that it contributed towards the abolition of the death penalty in this country.

I thought I knew all the tricks of the trade when I arrived in Dartmoor. I was sure of myself, cocky, but the Moor soon disillusioned me. Beside some of the old hands I was a right mug. Just take the matter of smoking. In ordinary life it doesn't matter much whether your pals smoke or not, but in prison a cigarette can literally become a matter of life or death.

Behind the walls the craving for a smoke will get so bad that a man will sell his body and soul for a cigarette. Tobacco means power, and on the Moor and in Parkhurst that power is in the organised hands of the tobacco barons who are bookmakers and moneylenders. They even had a pawnshop. I've known men pawn their false teeth, banjos, mandolins, rosaries and even a cat. I've known a prisoner so desperate for a smoke that for half an ounce of tobacco they have exchanged their jam, cheese, butter and sugar rations for a month, with one jam duff a week thrown in. One prisoner doing three years for killing someone killed for the second time, not over a woman, not over money, but over a cigarette and one jam duff. For that he got ten years' penal servitude. If you were wise you chose non-smokers as your friends because they wouldn't shop you to an unscrupulous warder for a couple of snouts.

It was nothing to see a tobacco baron collecting four pounds of butter a week from his clients while the public outside the walls were on scanty war-time rations.

The tobacco baron in my time was Black Joe Kelly, a wrestler from Bradford, doing ten years for selling plans to the German

Embassy. Some of the men who couldn't pay their debts when the time came got into a terrible state. It was inevitable that they would receive a visit from the strong-arm mob and get a right belting, with sometimes a knife across their face. Terrified debtors would go to any lengths to avoid their chiv punishments. They would strike the jailer or commit some other offence to get put in solitary confinement. Many stayed in solitary confinement for more than six months because they were afraid of the knife. They swallowed knives, razor blades, nails and glass, cut their own throats, mutilated their bodies, and even hanged themselves in the hope of being transferred from the solitary cells to the hospital wing. On one occasion the fellow made a proper job of it by mistake. He timed it thinking that the jailers would open the cells from right to left, but on this particular day they opened up from left to right. By the time they reached him he was hanging dead.

Later, when I was at Parkhurst jail, Peter MacGowan, doing a twelve stretch for blackmail, was in debt to Benny from Leeds. He owed Benny the large sum of one pound and was given the ultimatum, "Pay up within twenty-four hours or else . . ." Peter failed to pay up. He was a tough, short little guy, in actual fact a slaughterer. It was decided that MacGowan should be cut with a cobbler's knife. Saturday afternoon was chosen when there was always a shortage of prison staff.

On Saturday afternoon MacGowan was playing dominoes in a gambling school in the association room. Benny was going to cut him from behind while both his hands were full of dominoes. The rest of the mob would cover up the chivving. They didn't mess about with him. There were only two officers in charge of about three hundred men that afternoon, and one of them was at the entrance of the cell block and couldn't leave his post. The other was his assistant and couldn't do anything alone in the general riot. Once the cutting had been done the chiv would be slipped from one prisoner to another. In the confusion Benny could duck through the crowd and back into his cell, establishing an alibi, and bang would close the door. The news was spread over the grapevine on Friday night. The tension in the block was obvious and there was a bigger crowd than usual round the dominoes school. Nobody spoke. Men shuffled uneasily and waited. Then it happened. Benny's left arm whipped out and around MacGowan's bent head, jerking it backwards. At the same instant his right hand slashed the cobbler's knife right across the man's face. MacGowan staggered to his feet, shaking the blood. His face had fallen apart from his mouth to his ear. The rest of the school smothered up and carried on as normal. A man steals your bird, or is a grass—kill the bastard. But how can you see anyone cut a man over a pound note without helping him? I went over to help him. I took him across to the hospital, but there was no doctor on duty. I started to cut him up through his pullover. It was in the winter. The medical officer arrived. He must have been standing behind me when I heard his voice.

"Have you finished, O'Connor?"

It was Dr MacDonald, a good man. He thanked me politely.

Back in the cell block they didn't find the chiv which had been tossed out of the window. For three months it lay jammed on the ledge unseen by the screws.

On my landing at Parkhurst at that time was a prisoner who I knew had not witnessed the MacGowan cutting. Not knowing his background, I had lent him my piano-accordion because he wanted to learn to play. He stayed locked in his cell all that afternoon and saw nothing, yet together with another prisoner who was doing ten years for rape they put their heads together and made up the story that they had witnessed the attack on Peter MacGowan. Hoping to get remission, they both gave evidence to the magistrates, but although this was a serious crime, the authorities decided to hush it up. Perhaps they knew a little bit about dubious evidence. In any case, Benny was not sent for trial.

The same man turned up again at the Hanratty trial as a witness for the prosecution. I met him in the street just after the trial and he tried to borrow a fiver off me. I told him I heard he'd committed perjury in the Hanratty trial.

"One of the coppers threatened to put it on me if I didn't," he said.

"You want to get a man hung because they threatened to put it on you?"

"Well, they threatened to charge me with murder."

I walked away.

During the trial I had, in fact, already informed counsel for the defence for Hanratty, Sherrard, that this prosecution witness was a professional perjurer. Such animals do exist.

8

A great knife slash down each cheek

The conditions on the Moor in the early 1940s were harsh and bad. They were certainly not conducive to reform. The Moor remains an evil place today. No lag was ever liable to improve his standard of education by association with the type of prison officer who drifted into the service during the war years. Many of these men admitted to me openly that they had become jailers to avoid war service, and the fear of losing their jobs and being drafted into the armed forces made them more zealous. Some were not only illiterate, but also sadistic. Hundreds of prisoners were always on report for breaches of discipline and the petty offences could be so construed by an officer eager to put himself right with his superiors. After the Home Office gave orders to tighten up Dartmoor, the war dodgers excelled themselves to put men on report. Those jailers in the profitable smuggling racket were the worst. They had to keep up a front and could only achieve that by having more men on report than their brother jailers. They gave false evidence against prisoners who were being adjudicated. Some of the diabolical crimes for which men were put on a bread-and-water diet were for feeding the jackdaws when the Moor was cold with snow, toasting a piece of bread, being in possession of the *News of the World*, borrowing a dictionary, being in possession of a cigarette while at labour. Conditions during the day were equally bad. There was little or no attempt at vocational training. Most prisoners were employed making hammocks, coal bags, mats and the inevitable mailbags. The outside parties worked in the market garden, or on land-reclaiming on the Moor, or the quarry. When the mist came down they were brought in to sew mailbags in a damp, dirty, unheated, disused hall. During working hours we weren't allowed to talk, however monotonous the job. These conditions finally led to revolt. At exercise one day several older prisoners approached me. I had just come out from the chokie cells. They knew I was feeling sore and didn't care. They told me something had to be done about these conditions, that they were quite prepared to have a go, and I had been chosen to lead. I was young. It seemed to me something of an honour to have been chosen to be the leader of these older tougher lags. I didn't realise they were using me as a mug, and listened to what they had to say. They told me that the deputy governor was responsible for the harsh discipline which had landed me in the strong cells. The plan was that in a couple of days' time, at a tally parade, I should seize the deputy governor and do him up. It would be the signal for a general riot and a prison break. Full of the plan, I talked to Ruby Sparks, a notorious escaper and something of a hero to us all. I knew I was safe. Ruby would never shop anybody. He was a veteran of the 1932 mutiny.

"Don't be a mug, kid," he said. "It's not worth it. There's only one way to do your life sentence: do it your own way, on your own. Believe me, you won't get away with nothing. Those so-called pals of yours, you can take it from me, they'll let you down when it comes to the push."

I wouldn't listen, but next morning I was called into the governor's office. The deputy governor was in the chair. Eventually, eyeing me not unkindly, he started to talk.

"O'Connor, I know all about it. You're going to attack me tomorrow and that's going to start a mutiny. Don't try it. You're young. You'll be in serious trouble. One move and we'll be waiting for you."

I stared at the wall behind his desk. "I don't know what you're talking about."

He smiled and took a strip of toilet paper from the drawer of his desk. There was writing on it. The deputy governor began to read. The full details of the plan had been given to him. He put his hand over the signature and looked at me again. "You've been grassed. My advice to you is to go away and think things over."

That night the prison officers began an intensive search of the cells. They found nothing with me, but in other cells they discovered chivs, coshes, escape material, and if they couldn't find it they stuck it there. A number of men went to the solitary cells. I did eventually discover who had shopped me. The man later hanged himself in his cell over a debt. After this experience I chose my pals more carefully.

I still continued to fight to prove my innocence and at the end of 1942 received a letter out of the blue from a firm of solicitors saying that they had been instructed by a Mr Jack Crawford to act for me. I did not know Jack Crawford, but knew many of his family and also that he was a receiver. I felt sure he was doing this because he knew the real murderer. The solicitor visited me and I wrote and thanked Jack Crawford, but I had a funny feeling about him and felt full of despair at the prospect of serving a life sentence for a murder I hadn't committed. I decided to get myself some publicity on my own and on February 27th, 1943, made a false confession to the murder of a mythical girl. Chief Superintendent Thorp was sent to Dartmoor to investigate, but, ironically, while he was there the papers announced that the Secretary of State had re-opened my case. After less than a year of my sentence I thought I was getting somewhere. I admitted that my confession to the murder of the girl was false and insisted that a prison officer remain as witness that I had never confessed to the murder of George Alfred Ambridge. The Chief placed this on record. I trusted Thorp no farther than I could see him.

Two months later, in March 1943, the police came to see me again. This time they were happy to inform me that the managing clerk of the firm of solicitors retained by Mr Crawford was a crook and that Jack Crawford had not paid the counsel's fees. "Your managing clerk has been arrested and sent to prison." Nothing came of the Secretary of State re-opening my case. I was cynical. I didn't expect it with Thorp on the job.

In despair I only made things worse and worse. I have always been my own greatest enemy. Determined to keep my case open, I went to confession and gave Canon Ryan permission to inform the Home Office of the crimes I had confessed committing. I wrote to the Chief Constables of Wiltshire, Berkshire and Bath city, confessing to crimes in those counties, hoping that the odds were that no three Chief Constables would collude against me. The C.I.D. from Bath visited me and I gave the Inspector a jewelled tiepin which I had taken from the jeweller's shop in Bath city to return to the owner, Mr Littuar. I told him that he could get the watch and chain from the Home Office and give it back to Mr Littuar as well. I warned him that Thorp was a villain and had suppressed facts. He was shocked, praised the integrity of police constables and said I would be out in a few weeks. I got out in three weeks all right, with ten years on top.

In July 1943 I got a job in the library. The governor warned the deputy governor, who had given me the job, that I would be back in the punishment cells inside a week. When he saw me pushing the barrow load of books I heard him make a crack to the chief, "He thinks he's pushing flowers along the Edgware Road."

But I lasted much longer than the governor thought I would. By intensive reading I began to enlarge my scanty education. My outlook on life began to change. I spent two years as a librarian.

Then the Prison Commissioners decided to turn Dartmoor into a prison for first offenders and court martial cases. All long-term prisoners were ordered to Parkhurst and I had to go with them. It was July 1945 and we left Dartmoor in prison clothes.

When we arrived at Portsmouth dockyards to take the ferry across to the Isle of Wight the quayside was full of gawpers. Not only were all the lifers handcuffed, but we had a long chain running through us. We were taken aboard the ferry in batches of two hundred. I had my head bowed to avoid the faces of the morbid onlookers. I felt like Guy the gorilla in Regents Park.

Crossing on the ferry, I asked one of the crew to bring the captain down. "Are you the guv'nor of this boat?"

"Yes," he said.

"You know there are mines in this channel?"

"Yes."

"Do you realise us lifers here will die like rats if we hit one?"

There was a row between a prison officer and the captain. The captain agreed with me and ordered the handcuffs and chains to be taken off of us lifers. That chief didn't forget me.

We were all feeling pretty dejected when we arrived at the Isle of Wight. Hundreds of holidaymakers watched us on the short train journey from Ryde Pier. I shall never forget first seeing Parkhurst Prison from the coach that brought us from Ryde. The warm red brick buildings and flower beds cheered me up after the grey granite at Dartmoor. The chief medical officer was good old Dr MacDonald. The chief officer, Jack Hunt, known as 'Mad Jack', was at the gate as the coaches rolled in. He gave us a cheery smile. We couldn't believe it.

Nothing like this had happened to us before. Inside was the same bright atmosphere. After a thorough medical check up, I went to my cell. It had a wooden plank floor, a spring mattress bed, and, wonder of wonders, a steam radiator. Even the white-and-green walls, standard to all British prisons, looked cheerful and different, and the cell's electric light was a change from the gloomy gaslamps at Dartmoor. To cap it all, a radio in the cell block was playing music.

The first time I saw a Parkhurst prisoner I couldn't believe it. He was wearing a smart white shirt which had been bleached, a pair of neatly hand-pressed trousers, highly polished well-made shoes. He looked more like a respectable business man than an old lag. I went to sleep that night feeling great.

Not long after we arrived, the bookmakers and the racketeers were about again. At the weekends we had football, something unheard of at Dartmoor, and there was soon a gambling school in operation on the touchline. A large-scale football pool was started in opposition to the Scottish mob, and the London mob set up a horse-racing combine. With the cash that was flowing their way they corrupted the cookhouse and lived like lords while the mugs went on short rations. Even if one of the strong boys was sent to solitary confinement he still got better food than the ordinary prisoner, and supplies of butter, jam and other luxuries were smuggled into the top-security wing. Ironically, the prison was a store for the Ministry of Food during the war. The stuff that was nicked out of there; jailers, the lot, all helped themselves.

The Prison Commissioners unknowingly helped the rackets along. In the interests of wartime economy they ordered that no food should be weighed before issue. No prisoner could therefore complain he hadn't received his full ration of meat or butter, even though he knew that three-quarters of his portion had gone to the heavy mob or the screws. Complaining was dangerous. A prisoner who beefed about anything was liable to get a visit from the heavy mob in the early hours of the morning while the warders were distracted.

There were three different firms in Parkhurst jail, the Scottish mob, the Northern mob and the London mob. I was a lone wolf and had the religious bug at that time. There was always a needle between the three firms. The Northern mob had a row with a character called Scarface Jock. One day in the compound at exercise I saw one of the Northern gangsters leaning against the wall talking to some of his pals. Then I saw Scarface Jock come up, watching the mob warily. He had already been warned what might happen. As he drew level with the group by the wall the Northerner ducked through his mates and grabbed Jock, pushing him on to the football field. As the two men went down I saw the knife, but the other gangsters milled around to hide them from the warders. A second later the mob dispersed. Jock had a great knife slash down each cheek and across his forehead. He squared up bravely, but he couldn't see to fight whoever it was. Someone grabbed him and took him to the hospital. He had to have forty-eight stitches.

A few moments later I was stopped by a smooth grey-haired man known as the Conning Major. He asked me what had happened.

"Someone's been cut."

"What with?"

"What do they usually cut people with?"

Half an hour later, on the way back to my cell, another prisoner stopped me and asked what had happened. I told him that someone had cut Scarface Jock. He thought for a moment and then said, "Well, if no screws saw it, nobody can be convicted."

"They could," I said, "if a few informers get to work, which no doubt they will."

At seven o'clock the same evening my opponent in the chess tournament was the gangster who had cut Scarface Jock. We played the first game in silence. During the second game I said, "Have you got anything in your cell that you could be nicked for?"

"No," he said.

"Look, take notice of me. They'll nick you for sure tomorrow morning under some pretext." The following morning he was charged with being in possession of a pair of eye tweezers found in his cell, and that was sufficient to put him in the punishment block, now the maximum-security block at Parkhurst where Richardson and the Krays are held. Inside a week he was taken to the magistrates' court and charged with the attempted murder of Scarface Jock.

As I left for work I saw the Conning Major, the other prisoner who had asked me about the cutting, and a third man being bundled into a car wearing civilian clothes and with their wrists handcuffed. A pal told me, "They're witnesses for the prosecution in the cutting case."

I was a bit taken aback. "How the hell can they be witnesses? They were nowhere near the cutting."

The next day I applied to see the governor. I told him I wanted to see the solicitor defending the man who had attacked Scarface Jock.

"You wish to make a statement?" asked the governor cautiously.

"No, in the interests of the man accused of attempted murder, I'll talk to nobody but his solicitor." He had to grant my request and in due course I appeared at Winchester Assizes as one of the defence witnesses. I told the court that I was no particular friend of the defendant. Whether he was guilty or not guilty was for the jury to decide. What concerned me was perjury. I knew that the Conning Major and his friend were lying, committing perjury, when they said they had seen the cutting, and I was not prepared to see a man shopped or convicted on perjured evidence, even if he was guilty. Mr Justice Charles seemed impressed and warned the jury that some of the prosecution witnesses might not be entirely reliable. The Northern gangster was found not guilty. In fact, I had committed perjury, but I was prepared to do that rather than see a man convicted on perjured evidence.

Parkhurst hospital was called the halfway house to Broadmoor. It is a red-brick three-storey building apart from the main prison with, then, two open wards, some cells including a special tuberculosis landing, and padded cells for refractory cases and those on their way to Broadmoor. There was a strange collection of men in the hospital. I worked in the library and used to take books over to the patients.

A blood feud landed Hue Leung, aged twenty-four, in the dock at Manchester. One day in Hong Kong, Leung's mother told him that his father had been poisoned and robbed of fifty thousand dollars by a civil servant called Chang Ling Fok. Leung swore revenge. Chang became a seaman. Leung followed Chang from Hong Kong to Liverpool and in a Chinese seamen's club stabbed his father's killer fatally with a wooden-handled knife. A Chinese waiter who saw the killing told the court, "When I knew he was avenging his father I walked out of the club."

Leung was a likeable little man. He couldn't read English, so I used to bring him picture books. He'd sit all day in his cell turning the pages and crooning some Chinese song to himself. He lived in a world of his own, and when he wasn't looking at the picture books he used to make beautiful lampshades. We were all glad when finally some Chinese who had been convicted of robbery with violence were sent to Parkhurst. We thought that poor lonely old Leung would be laughing and happy at last. We couldn't have been more wrong. Inside a week there was blue murder. They set up a fantan game. Every time someone lost there was another fight. In the finish they all ended up in chokie. The screws weren't standing for Tong warfare.

Another so-called murderer who interested me and who also couldn't read or write was Joe. I was in the hospital for two or three weeks with a bout of rheumatoid arthritis. The wide boys used to call Joe 'Hay and Straw'. They laughed at his Devon dialect. He had a soft voice and had been a labourer on a sheep farm. He had been inside for years for strangling a girl. He hid her body in a haystack.

I occupied my spare time studying criminal behaviour, murderers, blackmailers, gangsters and rapists. I was looking for the soul of man in the only material available. I found a simple soul in Joe 'Hay and Straw'. I knew the torment of not knowing when you'll go out and wondering whether you'll die in jail. My sympathy always lay with the lifers.

One day I was sitting at the table in the association hospital room having my lunch. There were about a dozen round the table: Robbie, a lifer; Billy, who killed three birds; Nobby, who shot his wife's lover; Joe 'Hay and Straw'; and Wally, who strangled a prostitute for giving him a dose of the pox. He always said he had lost his temper with her when she refused to give him back his thirty bob. I looked round the table. Between us we had done a hundred years. Nobby spoke first.

"Any news today?"

I took a spoonful of bubble and squeak and said, "Yes, Taffy's got his date." When a lifer gets his date there's always a little bit of jealousy, especially from those who've already done twelve years. In chorus they said, "Good luck to him, good luck to him."

Joe looked really sad and unhappy. He said he'd like to talk to me when I finished my meal. I moved from the table and Joe joined me.

"Well, Jim," he said, "first of all, would you see if you can get me some more picture books. I've seen nearly every picture book in the library. I'd like some pictures of horses and rivers."

"I'll do my best, Joe, when I get out of hospital." I knew Joe could hardly read and no one had ever tried to teach him. He received no letters. He had no living relative. He did jigsaw puzzles in his gate cell and talked to the birds.

"I know they call me Hay and Straw," he said, "but there's nothing better than the beautiful fields of Devon, with rivers where trout and salmon jump in the weirs." When I accused him jokingly of being a poacher, he was up in arms. "I'll have you know I'm a Plymouth Brother, and so was Farmer Baxter who I worked for. No, I wouldn't kill a trout or any fish. They're all God's little creatures."

When I said, "What about God's little creature that you strangled in the haystack?" he nearly cried.

"I never meant to kill her. That's another thing I want to talk to you about. It's like this. I've worked inside the jail for twelve years as a gardener, but you know I love horses and cows. They won't let me go to work on a farm. Why? You know I can see a sheep farm from the window of my cell on the top of the hill. All I want to do is to be with horses. You know, of course, that horses love me and we talk to each other. Now when I was a little boy I worked for Farmer Baxter and did right up till the time I was in prison. He was a good man. He gave me fifteen shillings a week and promised me a horse of my own."

Joe was still getting fifteen shillings a week when he was arrested at thirty-two years of age. Farmer Baxter had indeed found a simple soul.

A jailer came into the dining-room and called out, "Anyone for the Salvation Army meeting?" Joe got up to go.

I said, "I thought you were a Plymouth Brother."

"I am," said Joe. "But the Salvation Army have promised me that when I get out, they'll get me a job on a farm looking after their horses, and the captain has a horse of his own, so I'll go and play with them and talk about horses. God knows I love horses."

I played some chess with Nobby for an hour; then Joe came back.

"Can we have a talk?"

"Of course." So I took him into a corner.

"Well, as I was saying, do you think that you could write a petition to the Home Secretary and ask him to let me go out and work on the Salvation Army farm?"

"Of course," I said. "Before I can write a petition I have to know more about the girl in the haystack."

"Well," he said, "I told no one this, but I'll tell you. I'd never been with a woman before, you see. I had never left the country. I worked from five in the morning till ten at night. We were cutting hay and the girl was camping in the next field. She was pretty. I asked if she could help me haymaking. She asked me about cows and bulls and how did cows make love and asked me to show her. I promised I would one day. I sat behind the stack drinking cider. She came and kissed me and asked me to do to her what the bull did to the cow. I told her I didn't know how to. She said she'd show me, and she did. I'd never done it before. It was very nice. I liked it. I did it again and again, and then she told me to stop. But it was nice. I didn't want to. She slapped my face. I pushed her away, and they say she was dead."

"Tell me, Joe," I said. "Did you appeal against your death sentence?"

"Oh, no. I mean, I knew they wouldn't hang me because I told them I'd never done it before. Anyway, I thought they'd fine me five shillings."

I thought you must be joking. Anyway, I petitioned the Home Secretary on Joe's behalf and said that he had no previous criminal record. He had spent twelve years without breaking a prison rule and was not likely to become a menace to society.

Six weeks went by before Joe got a reply. It said the contents of his petition had been noted and would be considered when his case came up for review. This, of course, meant no luck. But Joe, he thought they were thinking about letting him out. "You told them I loved horses, Jim?"

"Of course. The Home Secretary loves horses himself."

"He must be a good man then," said Joe. "Not like Prince Philip and the Prime Minister. They just like shooting birds. I wouldn't ask them to let me out. I don't like them."

I missed Joe the next day. He'd been transferred to another ward. After a week I went and saw Joe. He was very excited. "What do you think, Jim? I'm going out tomorrow. I'm going to the Salvation Army farm with the horses." Joe was a happy man indeed. "I won't need your books, but thanks," he said.

I left the hospital feeling very happy for Hay and Straw. I was determined not to miss waving goodbye to him in the morning. He knew my cell window and had to pass it on the way to the gates where he would walk out to freedom. Good old Joe. I stood on my cell stool early next morning to be sure not to miss waving Joe goodbye.

I saw him coming down the drive in his shabby brown suit. He was getting nearer. He called out to me, "Goodbye, Jim, God bless you," in a laughing voice. When he got to the gate he turned and waved at me, smiling, but it was a wave with a difference. He was waving with two hands joined by handcuffs. A lump came to my throat as I called out, "Goodbye, Joe, God bless you." After twelve years he was on his way to Broadmoor Lunatic Asylum.

I never thought Joe was a murderer and I wasn't alone in my view. At his trial at the Assizes the defending counsel asked the officer in charge of the case, "Did you at one time suspect someone else of being guilty of this murder?"

And the officer had answered, "Yes."

The counsel persisted, "Do you still suspect someone else?"

And again the Detective Superintendent said, "Yes."

Why then did Joe confess to the killing of the girl and hiding her body under the haystack? My answer to that is simple. Poor Joe was a nut. Many people confess to murders they haven't committed. Unfortunately, this was one confession the police couldn't disprove. Joe was convicted. It beats me why he was ever sent to Parkhurst to serve all those years as an ordinary prisoner when even at his trial it was evident he was crazy. Dr Dickson, the prison doctor, told the court that four of his relatives were in mental homes. He added, "Not the slightest reliance can be placed on anything he says." According to medical evidence, Joe had the mind of a child of twelve. He actually thought that he would be fined five shillings on the charge of murder he was facing. There was no evidence against him except his own statement and it was not the first time he had accused himself of murder. Poor old Joe. I hope they've got horses in Broadmoor.

There was a grimmer side to Parkhurst hospital. Men dying of tuberculosis were not allowed in the open wards. They were cooped up in cells with locks and iron bars, no different from the ordinary prison cell except for a small open grating in the door. If they were bedridden and unfit for exercise, they stayed in their cells twenty-four hours a day. No wonder they were irritable. Continual brooding can drive sick men to attacking warders, or trying to destroy themselves. The nursing staff, although not highly qualified, were reasonably humane. Many were kind enough to open the cell doors of these dying men so they could forget their troubles in the pleasure of a little bit of conversation with their pals. As a librarian I could walk in and out of their cells as I liked, but this concession, which should be introduced officially by the prison authorities, would end abruptly when the lookout man called out, "The Slug's arrived."

The Slug was an officer at the hospital who terrified and humiliated the nursing staff. He believed in discipline and rule by fear. A little man with a mouthful of bad teeth and a false smile, he was the most hated and despised jailer I knew, and even wore heavy boots with thick leather soles, no doubt nicked out of the shoe shop and the nearest he could get to jackboots.

If any of the dying men got near putting themselves right with God, they changed their minds as soon as the Slug appeared. He brought the hate from the bottom of their boots. I heard one nurse, a cheerful little cockney called Williams, being given a lashing down by the Slug for making a sick man laugh. "That," said the Slug, "constituted familiarity with prisoners."

But Parkhurst was fortunate in having two good men, Dr MacDonald and Dr Angus. I don't know whether Scotland specialises in humanitarians. I only know that I've always found Scottish doctors kind to prisoners.

Prison doctors were not usually psychiatric specialists although they often had men under mental observation in their care. In fact, some of the prisoners were as well advanced in psychiatry as their doctors. They got hold of the books of Freud, Adler and others and studied them in their cells. Sometimes they learned so much that by faking the necessary symptoms they managed to get themselves transferred to the comparative luxury of Broadmoor. The doctors didn't know enough to spot a fake, or if they did, they didn't care.

Jail was a home from home for queers. They used lipstick and rouge from the dye of red-covered books and bleached their hair. A friend of mine was a medical orderly. He had been in Broadmoor, he had been everywhere; a tough bastard, he cared for no one, but every time he broke out of jail he used to spend a thousands pounds on classical records and books on Nijinsky. We decided to find out which gangsters were queer, not the obvious ones but the secret and cunning ones. His job was following the medical officer round the landing with a tray round his neck containing various medicines; mixed aspirin, which is aspirin with water and given for most complaints, as well as various creams and ointments. He also had a good trade in a special cream known as "Starter" by the homosexuals and sold at fourpence a box. On this occasion he put an irritant in the cream. We waited until the next day and the day after to see who was complaining of having a sore bottom, and were amazed to discover the number of tough guys and gangsters who were affected. It is ironic that today two members of the government can bugger each other legally, but if two prisoners in a maximum-security prison are found doing the same thing they will be charged in front of magistrates and punished.

I used an informer to tell the governor that James O'Connor, the lifer, had photographs of homosexuality inside the prison. Black Joe, the governor, had worked his way up from the ranks and it was his first time as governor of a hard, tough convict jail. Then I set out a petition to the Secretary of State about the state of affairs in Parkhurst jail, the brutality and corruption amongst the screws and how they nicked the prisoners' grub. This caused a bit of a huff because it was virtually impossible for a governor to suppress a petition, and Black Joe certainly didn't want this one to go to the Home Office. He wanted them to be under the impression that everything was in order in the jail he was in charge of. He sent the principal officer to see me. He was a smooth-talking bastard. I was down in the punishment cells for refusing to go to labour. He came in to me all smiles.

"O'Connor, the governor's very disturbed about the contents of the petition. What is it you want?"

"What is it I want?" I replied. "Nothing." But they already knew that I had been smuggling letters out to the press which could be embarrassing to the governor and which also concerned my innocence of course.

The chief put a proposition to me. "O'Connor, tear this

petition up and let me go back to the governor and say you have withdrawn this petition, and then you can have any job that you want in this jail."

"Any job?"

"Yes, any job you want."

"I'll think about it," I said. "Come and see me after lunch." I thought about it. I thought this must be a weak governor. I'll take advantage of him. The chief came back.

"Yes," I said. "I'll be the governor's valet. I want complete freedom. I don't want to be a trusty, but I want the privileges of a trusty." This meant I could walk about and do what I liked and didn't have to wear a trusty's red band. A red band meant you had given the governor your word not to escape or abuse the trust placed in you. I got the job. It was a unique job in the history of penology.

I was on the pay roll as administration cleaner, but that covered a multitude of sins. At six o'clock in the morning I lit fires in the governor's office and the chief's office and made tea for the administration staff. I collected the newspapers from the gate and delivered them to the chief screw's office. As his messenger I had access to three parts of the prison. I collected diet sheets, medical restriction book, returned food records, the governor's application book, and visiting book. It was strictly a job for a warder. No prisoner should ever have been allowed to handle any of these confidential documents. I even had my own private office. It was as good as the governor's, in fact better, with a big coal fire and my own grill. I could walk in and out of the governor's office which was more than any of his screws dared to do, and I wore a tailored blue suit as good as any civilian sports wear, a white starched shirt which I changed twice a day, and hand-made brown suede shoes given to me by the doctor because of my two arthritic toes.

While I was in the governor's office I used to take off the top of his desk to look at the records he kept in there, those that he was dealing with at the moment. The others were in the strong room. I was able to read these while he was out watching football. He always watched football on Saturday and Sunday afternoons for two hours. I was able to read with interest reports on prisoners, reports on jailers, prisoners' reports on prisoners, jailers' reports on their brother officers and even petitions by prisoners to the Secretary of State. I discovered who all the informers were and knew more about what was going on in the prison than the best-informed warder, sometimes more than the governor himself.

The biggest shock I got was when I saw my own name on a 705A, a confidential report by senior officials on prisoners which is not only covered by the Official Secrets Act but by the Law of Privilege. The 705A can be a very libellous document. Mine was written in 1942 and signed by the deputy governor who had only seen me for five minutes. It read, "This man is a scoundrel. His expressed intention of living a straight life would be short lived." That document followed me through my entire prison history. It was taken into consideration each time my case came up for review for release, which was every four years. The first review at four years could be written off and forgotten about. Towards the eighth year there was hope. Towards the twelfth we felt despondent. I did not mind being called a scoundrel by this deputy governor. What hurt me was that a man who had seen me so briefly could bring himself to send such a document. I wondered how many other men had been condemned to serve years more than they need on such flimsy evidence. I tore the thing up.

After this I made it my business to read other confidential documents and reports on prisoners. Some were staggering. "This man will die on the scaffold." "This man is a street-corner boy who is likely to spend the rest of his life in prison." How could sane and sensible men bring themselves to make such sweeping and damning forecasts? In actual fact, the street-corner boy never returned to jail after that first sentence. Today he is a hard-working owner of a prosperous flower shop, and as for the man who would "die on the scaffold", in 1969 I saw him walking down the Portobello Road, the district he came from, in the robes of a monk. He was on leave from the Order he belongs to up the Amazon River.

I wish some of the prison informers could have seen the reports that their squealing had earned them. "This man will do anything to curry favour with the authorities. He exaggerates the slightest incident and creates situations where none exist." An informer is despised even by the men who make use of his information. It is amazing the number of gangsters looked up to and respected by other criminals who were informers.

My freedom of movement eventually led to my transfer from

Parkhurst under a cloud. Important documents relating to I.R.A. prisoners serving fifteen and twenty years were found missing from the files of another prison. There was a Home Office enquiry. The Home Office gave an order that in future no prisoner would be allowed to work in an administration building unless under the surveillance of a prison officer. My job was taken away from me. The governor called me, full of apologies. He had no alternative. It was a general order, not only for Parkhurst, but for every jail in England.

I was given another job, a job I refused to take, so I was punished for refusing to go to labour. By this time I had chronic rheumatism. Dr Mathison visited me in the maximum-security block at Parkhurst and had me transferred to the hospital. Then a Home Office order came to transfer me back to Dartmoor, now turned back into a jail receiving the toughest criminals in Great Britain. Against the prison doctor's advice, I was sent back to Dartmoor branded as a recalcitrant thug who would not respond to decent treatment.

9

The Bomber

If I wasn't pleased to see Dartmoor again, the prison was no more eager to see me. I found that out on my first interview with the governor. He told me frankly that he was sorry to see me back. The prison was now filled with youngsters who were serving long sentences for the first time. I was the only lifer among them and had the reputation of being a tough customer. These youngsters had no previous experience of the Moor. The governor said that they were serving their time quietly. There was every hope that many of them would straighten themselves out if they were left alone. He didn't want an old lag like me making trouble for them. I could understand his point of view. Major Harvey had only recently been appointed governor of Dartmoor. According to grapevine information, he was a square shooter and a sincere and humane man. Already he had made reforms in the prison organisation. It was a different Dartmoor to me, and he was backed by a staff very different from that I had known during my previous stay there. Most of his warders were newly demobilised servicemen who had been through the war and who were just starting their careers, taking whatever jobs they could and anxious to do their best by the prisoner. You had the feeling that if you played straight with them they would do the same with you, and there were no more kickings and beatings.

I told the governor, none too politely, that I didn't need to start trouble, that as far as I was concerned Dartmoor was only an inconvenience to me. I planned to cultivate him and get myself an opportunity to escape. I was bitter and had a chip on my shoulder. I had had enough of being in prison for a murder I had not committed. Having already served a number of years the hard way, I knew most of the answers and if I wanted to be awkward I could beat them with my head, my knowledge of prison rules and regulations. I said I neither wanted nor needed to resort to violence. As long as I was left alone, treated decently and got what I was entitled to, he would get no trouble. He wouldn't even know I was in the prison. He nodded with an amused glint in his blue eyes. "All right, and what do you think you are entitled to?"

"Freedom of association and the right to play my accordion in my cell; some books, because I am studying, on philosophy and psychology, which were in my property but were taken away when I was received in the jail."

"Well, you'll be wanting drums next week." Then after a short pause he said, "Very well, you can have your accordion and your books."

To his surprise, however, I took no advantage of my association privileges. I stayed in my cell. I was happy enough with my writing and my own thoughts. I studied the 'isms' again. I suppose I was purging the catharsis, my own catharsis, purging myself, examining myself. I started my first, attempted, serious writing.

One evening I was in my cell writing a play, a thirty-minute play. I used to write one every weekend to pass away the time. The governor came into my cell.

"Look here, O'Connor, you kicked up enough fuss about freedom of association when you first came in. Now you never go near the Association Room. What's the trouble?"

"I'm better on my own," I said. "I've got plenty to do here. Writing is a lonely job."

He sat down on the edge of my bed. I was sitting in the corner, writing. For a minute there was silence. Then he said, "You know, O'Connor, you could help us a lot by going down to the Association Room. There's only half a dozen youngsters over there and a couple of newly arrived lifers. They just sit around there twiddling their thumbs and brooding, and they need someone to organise their recreation. For example, there's a man who wants to play chess. I understand you're a very good chess player."

"Well," I said, "let him find a partner."

"He can't. There isn't one among them."

"Well then, teach somebody."

The governor went on talking. Eventually I agreed to go across to the Association Room. It was on the first floor of a small part of the main prison. When I walked into the room I knew why the prisoners could raise no enthusiasm for their privileges. The room was cold, cheerless, colourless, dirty. The beige distempered walls were cracked and peeling, with damp running down. The bare floor was filthy, and the once white-washed ceiling was grey and flaking. Two naked gas jets supplied the only illumination. For furniture there was a table and plain kitchen chairs. The eight men on association, none of them serving less than ten years to life, were sitting around talking gloomily. As far as I could hear, the only topics were their sentences and the tough conditions under which they were serving them, because as soon as they saw me they crowded round, shook hands, poured out their complaints and asked me for advice. A lot of those youngsters looked up to me. I was just then turning into a cunning barrack-room lawyer, and told them to use their loaf, use their nut, use their brains. Brains were always better than brawn.

Their grouses were various. They had been deprived of Sunday newspapers, were sleeping on bedboards instead of the spring beds they should have been given after completing the first four years of their sentence. They had no facilities for outdoor sports or indoor recreations. Of one set of chessmen, half the pieces were broken or missing. There was nothing to do in there except sit around and talk. Even the antique radio set was out of order one week in four because of the shortage of batteries. The night staff used to sleep on a couple of beds in the room. In breaks they listened to the radio and the batteries were knocked out.

I promised to do what I could. That evening I saw the governor and pointed out the condition of the room. "How would you like to live in a place like this?"

"I know," he said. "It's terrible, but there's nothing I can do. The maintenance of the building is the affair of the Foreman of the Works and the Steward, and they are limited by the amount of money the Government gives them to spend."

"Oh, Governor, that's a lot of old nonsense. Look, never mind the foreman. Give us a few buckets of paint and we'll give you a surprise." He agreed, and we cleaned the place down and painted it, armed with distemper, green paint and a good supply of soap and water. Saturdays and Sundays we scrubbed, rubbed and polished. The boys forgot to brood over their troubles.

The governor gave one of the prisoners permission to teach us bridge, which meant he gave us access to playing-cards. Of course, he turned a blind eye. He knew we were playing solo or rummy. When we were not playing cards I used to take the accordion over there and play at night time. The night patrol officers who used the room after we were locked in our cells could not believe their luck. They now had a nice place to kip in.

I have always basically been a loner and only like doing things I can do on my own. When I was told that the stoker was being released from the stokehouse, I decided that I had done my brain quite a bit of good over a period of years and would now get my body physically fit again. Maybe plenty of hard work would cure my rheumatics. I applied for the job, got it, and was told I could start work when the man doing it was released in three or four weeks' time.

In the meantime I went into hospital because my knees and toes were swollen from arthritis. In hospital, where an old friend from Parkhurst, Nobby, was orderly, I kept looking at the bars in my cell window. I noticed that one of them was about a quarter of an inch narrower. It was the last bar against the wall. I thought it might be an opportunity for me to escape. Facing was the moor and the sky and the grey low mist. I made an indentation in the wall and kept rubbing the stone, pounding it slowly and quietly.

A keeper, when I used to duck into the Regents Park Zoo, had told me that if my head went through the railings, my body would always follow. This was the theory I worked on. All my hair was cut off, and one lunch time when the mist came down I decided to go. I greased my body and my head with margarine that I had been saving up and vaseline I had got hold of. Then I started to wedge my head between the bars in the wall. The pressure on the scalp really hurt. Eventually my head was through, but the schoolboy theory didn't work out. My body wouldn't follow. There was I, stuck, with my head outside the bars, stark naked and covered with margarine. All of a sudden the door opened. Fortunately it was Nobby, who was very humane or maybe he was a bit dim.

"Here, what are you doing up there?"

"Nobby," I said, "I was feeding the birds. I've stuck my head out here. One's fallen down on a ledge. It's a baby bird. It's fallen on the floor now. I've missed it. And I've got stuck."

"You've got what?"

"I've got stuck. My head's stuck through here."

It must have been a funny scene if anybody was looking on. But it wasn't funny for me. I hope he believed me because I was bang in trouble if he didn't.

Nobby put his feet against the wall and his arms around my waist and pulled me back. The sides of my head were grazed and cut.

"You silly boy. Don't you ever do that again," he said.

"No, Nobby. No, Nobby. Go out and get that bird for me."

"Oh, I've got no time," he said. It was a good job he didn't look for it.

Anyway, my knees got slightly better. They came and asked me whether I thought I was fit to do the job. Despite this rheumatoid complaint I was quite strong. "Of course," I said. Again I was lucky. One of the Scottish doctors had been transferred to Dartmoor.

"Don't put the block on me getting this job. If I can't do it after a few weeks I'll let you know."

By the time I got to the stokehouse I had decided to use the system as it had used me. A double indemnity is sentence, never knowing whether you're going to die in Dartmoor, or if you will ever see your family. Never having visits from relatives is torture. My mother visited me now and again. In fact, she stuck to me, as all mothers always do, for the whole of my life sentence, but she was broke and I couldn't expect anything from her. Ironically enough, although she was unaware of the fact, she worked as charlady to a cat burglar in Chelsea who I knew very well. My first wife never ever visited me in Dartmoor jail, never even sent me a copy, twopence in those days, of *Picture Post.* I never ever saw my son while in prison, and spent many years thinking about them both. Later I learnt she was having an affair. I wished I had a brother or a sister or someone who could help me fight my case. I needed money. By being a stoker I could fiddle. With all the coal lorries coming in, the stokehouse was a good place to traffic from.

I found a crooked jailer. At that time the London Airport robbers had just come in after the Battle of Heathrow, when the coppers had ambushed them in the Valuable Cargo Shed. All these people needed looking after by the underworld outside the jail. Being a stoker, I had to work out a system.

I shifted fourteen tons of coal a day, and worked from half

past five in the morning until ten at night. The barrows I used were made of steel and carried about two hundredweight. I asked the master carpenter, a civilian, if he could make me a very lightly balanced barrow in which I could carry more coal, saving me some journeys to the boiler house. Of course, I gave him all the old cobblers about his engineering ability. Then I asked if two pals of mine working in the carpenter's shop could do the job. I used an informer named Little who was doing fifteen years for strangling a prostitute, to carry the contraband. The barrow stood outside the boiler house at night and I never came in contact with the crooked screw. He used to take out the bottom, put in tobacco, and remove fresh letters to be sent out.

Little would do anything. He was trying to get my job. He was the yard man and used to take my new wooden barrow over to the carpenter's shop to get sawdust for my engine room. He would virtually jump to attention when I spoke to him.

"I'll give you a bacon sandwich when you come back," I used to say. Away he'd go. Of course, he had no chance with the cockneys in the carpenter's shop. By the time he got his barrow over the pit full of sawdust and they had given him a cup of tea, they had fannied to him, kidded him, taken out the tobacco and put in some more envelopes, and then he was on his way back to the boiler house. I carried on using the barrow all day and left it outside for the jailer at night. It must have cost the underworld a hundred pounds a week to look after those people for many, many years, and I saved up a nice few quid.

But all good things come to an end. The chief officer, Reggie Read, O.B.E., a man who had thirty years' experience of handling old lags, tall, grey-haired and always smartly dressed, retired. A good listener, he knew every stroke in the book and put himself out to help long-term men do their bird. He had a warm spot for old lags. If I ever made a complaint on behalf of the long-timers he always tried to help us. There were plenty of sighs when we knew we were going to lose him. Conditions always depend on the chief officer because the rest of the jailers follow suit. Whenever a top jailer is going to be replaced in a convict station the cells and workshops buzz with fear and speculation. Experienced lags prefer to be governed by educated, cultured men of good breeding like ex-service officers, not men who have risen from the ranks of jailers. They prefer military men who are used to handling men the right way and can't help feeling that an ex-jailer will never accept the word of a prisoner. As a governor from the ranks once said, "If one of my officers told me that he saw you driving a Rolls-Royce around your cell I would have to take his word for it."

Reggie Read's successor was a bastard. Within twenty-four hours we knew he had arrived. He was such a tough disciplinarian that before long he earned the name, 'The Bomber'. This man was security minded. Within a short time he collected all the most persistent escapers on one landing under strict supervision.

Even Dartmoor's tough regulations didn't satisfy the Bomber. He tightened things up further. Each day there were new regulations, and the governor always leaves these things to the chief.

Right away when he visited our Association Room I knew he was going to be a bit awkward, and he was. Grim faced, he looked round the room, never even taking his hat off or saying hello, but paying particular attention to the unbarred windows.

"Get bars up on those windows tomorrow," he said to the screw with him. The following day they were covered with bars and steel mesh.

By the time you reach that special stage you get such pleasure from the open windows. The jackdaws used to fly in and even if there was a jailer in the room we used to feed the birds. I loved birds. I still do. Sometimes they'd fall out of their nests and hurt themselves. We would get them better so that they would be able to fly away. We always used to say that jackdaws were the souls of old lags who'd died and come back into the jail. One was called Jack Fogarty after an old lag who had died in the jail at the age of eighty-five. I even had my own pet jackdaw that I trained. He used to sit on my cat's back in the stokehouse. He could have flown away if he wanted to. I never clipped his wings. He either couldn't fly or he didn't want to fly. One day he was sitting on a coal bunker, while I was using a steel bar to raise the clinker in the boiler. He jumped and sat on the steel bar and the in-draught took him straight into the boiler. It was the end of my jackdaw.

My cat was a prize cat, a beautiful cat. I sold him to jailers two or three times for a few ounces of snout, but I had no worries. He always came back to me. He was the only one I knew who ever wanted to get into a nick. He found a way in, just walked in through the gate, and back he came to the boiler house. One screw beat me at my own game one day. He bought it off me and sent it off to relatives. It won a few prizes.

All the cats in the jail knew me. I never saw them until Sunday. I never knew where these cats went during the week but for sure on Sunday there would be thirty or forty lying outside the boiler house on the heated flagstones. Just after two o'clock I went round gathering from the top tins of five or six hundred prisoners, the remnants of their dinner. I used to put them in a tray and give them each as much as I could, keeping the rest so that I could feed my cat for the rest of the week.

The Bomber walked down the drive on a Sunday afternoon on his way to chapel, and I don't know who he prayed to because when he saw thirty or forty cats lying about chewing away at their meat he said, "Hey, you, stoker, drown that fucking lot."

I looked at him with contempt. "Drown them yourself. And don't swear at me. If you swear at me I can fucking well swear at you. You just leave me alone and I'll leave you alone. You're not going to drive me mad. You won't beat me."

He gave an order that all cats in the prison were to be drowned. That was the Bomber, always making trouble when everything was peaceful, long chin sticking out, thumbs tucked into two buttons by his lapels.

My next clash with him was over Timmy from my manor, only twenty-one and doing five-stretch. He gave me all the news from Paddington, who was in the army, who was out of the army, who was rich and who was poor, who was in the nick and who was out of the nick, who was married to who and who had children.

Timmy worked in the laundry. He was in constant trouble for breaches of prison regulations. I used to send tobacco down to the punishment cells for him, but there was one screw in particular who hated Timmy. He took a delight in riding him. Finally, Timmy retaliated in the only way he knew. He knocked him out with a right hook and to top it up he bit his nose. He was charged, convicted and automatically sentenced to twelve strokes with the birch.

The screw who was attacked had to be present when the prisoner who assaulted him was being beaten with the birch. Before flogging, this particular screw came into the boiler house and sat up at the top, hidden, smoking. Making out he was a good fellow, he offered me a cigarette. I was pleased to refuse.

I saw the governor with the doctor, the Bomber and four warders walk past the entrance. The jailer in the boiler house left and followed them. They were heading for the laundry. I felt sick. Everybody in the jail felt sick when the machines started up in the laundry to drown the screams of the prisoner.

At about half past two the Bomber came back alone. He walked into the boiler house carrying a birch wrapped up in a length of white cloth. Both were soaked with blood, Timmy's blood, a boy from Paddington, from my manor. He threw his bundle on the floor. "Burn that," he ordered.

I stared at him. "Not me, mate. You used the fucking things. You burn them. But let me remind you that there's a regulation that says you cannot use *my* furnace for burning rubbish. You have to take it to the incinerator. That's the engineer's instructions. These boilers have to be kept as clean as possible and they must only receive clean fuel."

He looked at me. I had him beat on regulations. Without a word, he picked up the birch and cloth, opened the furnace door and threw them in. Then he walked out. However much he wanted to charge me with insolence, he knew I was within my rights. He knew that that moment was no time for upsetting me or any other prisoner because when floggings are in the air men are very touchy and can get dangerous. I had a shovel in my hand and felt like smashing him across the head with it.

Apart from hangings, at no time were the prisoners so upset. They were locked in their cells about ten minutes before the flogging was due to begin. They were unlocked about half an hour after it was all over. During that time silence hung over the cells. The whole prison was listening. Even when the men were released for exercise they talked only in whispers. The warders in charge of them walked very warily. They knew the least spark could set off an explosion. It was a day before the restlessness subsided.

Before a flogging at Dartmoor the carpenter used to go to the laundry and erect the tripod and heavy wooden apparatus eight foot high, secured to the floor by iron rings. By the time he had finished, the governor and the chief prison officer had arrived. Soon afterwards the prisoner was brought from the punishment block by an escort of six or eight warders. He wore nothing but a shirt and trousers, socks and slippers. If he had been allowed to wear boots he might have been tempted to kick someone. The governor read the sentence imposed by the magistrates and confirmed by the Secretary of State. The man's shirt was removed and he was strapped to the tripod by warders, with his hands strapped above his head, his legs spread wide apart, ankles strapped and his head screened with a cloth to prevent him from seeing the man who was carrying out the flogging. A padded leather belt was also secured round part of his body to protect his kidneys and a white cloth was spread on the ground to collect the blood splashes.

The doctor, having already examined the man's heart and checked his fitness for punishment, stood in front of the tripod to check the victim's face during the ordeal. He gave a signal to the governor. The flogger was usually chosen from the strongest warders in the jail. He stepped from behind a screen and the punishment began. As the birch or cat of nine tails descended, the governor counted each stroke aloud.

The birch was a tight bundle of thin wooden strips, two inches in diameter, four feet long. The cat was a number of whipcord thongs about eight inches long secured to a short leather handle. Despite popular belief, there are neither knots nor lumps of metal on the thongs. Although the birch was supposed to be the lesser punishment, it was far more dreaded than the cat. Many prisoners who have tried both have told me, "I'd rather take twelve with the cat than six with the birch any day." But in the hands of a prison officer who enjoys his job, and most of them seemed to, either was a terrible instrument. The skin started to flay off a man's back after the first or second stroke. The toughest man I knew fainted after five strokes of the cat. When I discovered this, he was very concerned that I should tell no one that he had fainted. I did not.

When the prisoner was released from the tripod he was given first aid treatment on the spot, then taken to the hospital to have his back properly dressed, and within half an hour was back on exercise.

Some carried their scars for many years. Some old lags were having an argument one day and one man, to prove his point, ripped off his shirt. His back still bore clearly the scars of the flogging he received in Dartmoor jail in 1941.

I hear and read a lot about how flogging brutalised the men

who carried it out. I can only say there was never any lack of volunteers for the job although it only carried a couple of shillings by way of fee. It horrified me to see warders jockey for the chance of watching a flogging. The shed was always packed. I used to see them coming out afterwards, laughing and joking as if they'd been to a circus.

I have seen the heads of scores of prisoners and ex-prisoners criss-crossed with scars like a railway depot, evidence of the times they have been beaten with truncheons. A prisoner disobeyed an order to stop talking and was given three days' bread and water. As he left for the punishment block, the reception committee known as the Gestapo was there waiting to give him a right belting. I saw the warders chuck him headfirst down the polished steel staircase. Unconscious, he was thrown into a strong cell, a cell with two doors. Then *he* was charged with assaulting a prison officer. The charge had to be made to explain his extensive injuries. He got fifteen days' No. 1, bread and water; forty-two days Number 2, porridge and potatoes; three months' confinement to the solitary cells, and lost six months' remission of sentence. It was by no means an exceptional case.

So many maltreated prisoners in another prison petitioned the Home Office that they ordered an enquiry which lasted several weeks. The Committee of Visiting Magistrates to Dartmoor reported that the staff did not use more force than was absolutely necessary, but the enquiry had its effect. The prisoners had a better time until the heat died down.

I met some good screws, but too many believe that the only way to deal with prisoners is to use the truncheon or the boot.

In 1951 when Little Jackie Rosa was sentenced to five years for attacking a prison officer in a dispute over a pair of trousers, he had already received the cat on four occasions, twelve strokes twice and fifteen strokes twice. He went to the Old Bailey straight from weeks of solitary confinement. His counsel submitted to Justice Hallet that he was beyond corrective training. Psychologists and prison officials expressed themselves baffled by the violence of this man. I knew Jackie well. I could have enlightened them. His head was a mass of scars, the result of many prison beatings. Jackie did not forget an injury, even if it meant the cat. Sooner or later he settled accounts with the screw who had ill treated him, and that is the explanation of men like Jackie Rosa.

I had a short rest from the Bomber. After eight years I was allowed to go to a London prison for visits. My mother being a charlady, it was a long, expensive journey to Dartmoor. People in Princetown were antagonistic towards relations of prisoners. They could smell them and there would be no accommodation to offer.

At Wandsworth jail was one of the toughest governors who ever ran a prison, but this governor was as tough with his warders as he was with his prisoners. He used to walk around on his own, looking for trouble and taking the piss out of the prisoners. He got chinned many times.

No lag fancied a spell in Wandsworth. It was overcrowded, three in a cell and full of bugs. Prisoners were locked up for nineteen hours out of twenty-four, twenty-two hours on Saturdays and Sundays. The stench was unbearable. People thought I was crackers to volunteer to go to Wandsworth, even for only a month. But I wanted to see my son whom I hardly knew.

I was given a job in the Miscellaneous Stores and that's where I saw the noose boxes. I don't know what attracted my attention to that row of twenty black japanned boxes, but they fascinated me. I asked one of the storemen what they contained.

"That's the hanging kits," he said. Wandsworth was the distribution centre for hangmen's ropes. They were sent from the prison not only to other British jails, but to the colonies and even to Germany. Each black box contained a length of rope, eleven feet for a white man and thirteen feet for a black man, with all the rest of the hangman's grim paraphernalia. Some contained twin kits for a double hanging. Before executions, one of these boxes used to leave Wandsworth addressed to the governor of the prison concerned. Afterwards it was returned to the stores for reconditioning at a little shop in the Old Kent Road, and eventually re-used.

Harry, the storeman, a cockney and a very funny character, pointed out a box to me bearing the number six. "Take a look at that one, Jimmy," he said. "That's the lucky box. When we send that one out we can lay bets on it it won't be used. Nine times out of ten the man it's intended for gets a reprieve." I couldn't help wondering if that was the box they had sent to Pentonville for me.

Working with me was a character called Eugene Messina, a notorious vice king who for years controlled the foreign streetwalkers in the West End with his four brothers. He was a fat, sallow-skinned man of medium height with jet-black hair always groomed like a film star's. The nails of his soft white fingers were carefully manicured and he took extra care of his perfect teeth. His voice was low and musical and it was easy to understand why women were attracted to him. He worked beside me. Despite the vigilance of the jailers, he never stopped talking. He had only one subject—crumpet. I could see he was having a rough passage because no one likes ponces. But I spoke to him. I'd talk to the devil if I had the chance, because I'm interested in everything. He couldn't understand how a man like me could laugh serving a life sentence. "When you get out of here, come and see me. We'll have a big party with girls and champagne. We'll go to Paris. I'll show you a fine time. You'll have plenty of money."

After a month in Wandsworth I was glad to get back to Dartmoor, despite the Bomber. When Dr Mack saw me he said, "Christ, what's happened to you?" I had lost a stone in weight. "Well, how did things go?" he asked. "Did you see her?"

"No." I had had no visits from my wife.

"You'd better have a couple of days in hospital on glucose and some Eastern syrup and get yourself fit."

"No, no, no. I'll go back to the boiler house."

My father died just after I got back.

This upset me. What with my domestic situation, I started to brood, got depressed and stayed in my cell. I didn't bother to read or write. I went to work in the boiler house. My feud with the Bomber had become an obsession. At last I decided I'd fix him and I applied to see the Commissioners.

At nine o'clock one night, Taylor, the deputy governor, came and got me from the stokehouse. It was an unusual time to see a Commissioner. "The Commissioner wants to see you." I declined.

"I don't want my application."

"Well, come and see him, O'Connor. It may be in your favour. He has someone else with him from the Treasury who's going to take over the Prison Commission."

I walked into the governor's office. There was Captain Williams, nicknamed Nuts and Bolts. He had two false legs and had known me for years.

"Sit down."

He offered me a cigarette.

"No," I said, "I'll smoke my pipe."

"Well, O'Connor, what's the trouble?"

"Trouble?" I said. "That's a funny thing. I was all steamed up. To be honest, I was all set to give that chief a coating; but, you know, it doesn't seem to matter. I suppose the guy's got to do his job the way he sees it. That's what I wanted to see you about, but let's forget about him."

I had noticed a man sitting in a corner.

"I've been here longer than any man. Don't you think you can help me to get a date and give me some sort of hope? You know, five years' time or three years' time. At least something."

"Well, boy, there's nothing much we can do for you," he said. "You have to wait for the review as laid down by statute. Let's see. Have you had a review?"

"Yes, I've just had one turned down. Do you think you can transfer me to one of those open prisons, the new ones?"

He listened to me sympathetically. "I'm sorry, O'Connor. I'm afraid we don't provide open prisons for men in your category. But I'll do my best for you. Now where else can we send you? What about Parkhurst? Would you like to go back there?"

"Well, at least it's got the sun record," I said, and thought it would get me away from the Bomber before I chinned him. "Yes, that will do me fine."

The Bomber thought he would give me no chance for villainy. "O'Connor for transfer in the morning. Don't tell him yet and don't unlock him for labour."

I packed up my piano accordion and had a screw carry it for me, but on the way I just popped into the boiler house to say goodbye. I nipped into the engine room lively and picked up a little hidden money. The two Gestapo came to see me in the cells. "O'Connor, we know you've been trafficking for a long time. Tell us how you were doing it."

"That's my secret. I'll tell you when I'm in the car with the handcuffs on me, on my way to Parkhurst."

They searched me. They turned me over, trying to find something on me. They found nothing. If they had taken my piano accordion to pieces they would have found money in each individual reed, but they never thought of that.

The Bomber said goodbye and wished me luck, smirking. I didn't answer him for a second, and then said, "Well, I've beaten you, haven't I? I've got away from your prison, mate." The inner iron gates swung open. The Gestapo was waiting there. The car stopped while they accounted and signed for the one body they were taking away from the jail. Then the outer gate opened. The Gestapo poked their heads into the car.

"What was it?"

"The wooden barrow, you pair of burkes! The wooden barrow outside the boiler house. Your informer has been pushing it about for ages for me."

10

"Love in the pissed"

Away we drove. I enjoyed the ferry ride on my own. The jailers took the cuffs off me. They didn't care. They knew I couldn't get away. I smoked. I was dressed in civilian clothes.

Parkhurst had changed. The prison was now filled up with new preventive detention men rated as incorrigibles. Ordinary penal servitude men were now being sent to other jails. Parkhurst was becoming known as the Old Lags' Home.

The most exclusive set in the prison were the forgotten men, old men who had been on preventive detention before the Criminal Justice Act was ever thought of, many of them over seventy years old. Looking into the cells of those veterans was like visiting a respectable almshouse; white-headed old boys sitting happily beside their radios, sucking their old pipes, carpet slippers placed neatly under the bed. On the wall might be a picture of the King or Queen, souvenirs of service in World War I. There would be bright curtains at the window and a carpet on the floor. A cat might be purring on the bed. A chew of tobacco or a cigarette, and then I'd sit there and listen. "This ain't a prison. It's a blooming convalescent home. In my days, boy, you used to have the old ball and chain round your leg. 'Face the wall,' when you come out of your cell. 'No talking.' They call this bird today. It's a lark."

Old Jack was the oldest burglar in England. He had no time for the modern cosh merchant. Like all old-timers, he despised young tearaways. "They haven't got the guts to stand up and have a clean fight. It was different in my day. We had to learn how to work proper. None of this here bashing old women on the head for a few bob. We used to get the old stick out, the jemmy, and work all night. We took pride in it."

One day I said, "What are you going to do when you get out, Jack boy? Get the old stick out again?"

"You bet," he cackled. "I'll show you young fellows how to do a nice clean job," and, believe it or not, he did. He was ninety years of age when he got out, and a month later he was back inside charged with being in closed premises and in possession of housebreaking implements.

Charlie the Creeper was another. He was about eighty and had done seven terms of penal servitude, including two tens, before starting on preventive detention. His trade was breeding kittens and selling them to old lags. He was the finest tomato grower the prison ever knew. Charlie was so attached to his little cell that he swore he would never leave Parkhurst. When finally his time was up they carried him down to the gates struggling desperately before they could get him into the motor-car which was to take him to freedom. Poor old Charlie never left the island. After a spell in St Mary's Workhouse, Newport, facing the prison, he contrived to get himself pinched for loitering with intent. Then he smashed the window of a shop and stole something. He didn't want to steal anything. He wanted to get back into Parkhurst. He missed his frying pan and all his old pals. He had no home to go to outside. They said he looked the picture of happiness as they put him back in the dock. His only worry was whether he would get back his own cell.

I must say the governor, Black Joe, wasn't too pleased to see me back. He gave me a job with two other lifers, Paddy Stewart and Robbie, working in the Miscellaneous Stores.

I met a little pal of mine from Notting Hill Gate. Jackie Worley was a little red-faced cockney and always had a cheerful smile. He had one passion in life, gambling. Even in prison he found ways of backing his fancy in the big racing events. One day while I was walking on exercise he told me he kept getting a shocking pain across his chest. "What do you suppose it is, Jim? Indigestion?"

"Could be. Don't take any chances."

"I go sick and all they give me is mixed aspirin," he said.

The pain continued, and a couple of days later he did see the doctor again. Again he gave him some mixed aspirin. Apparently his sickness wasn't taken too seriously. I went to his cell one day just before going to labour. I wanted to back a horse in the big race. As he bent down to put his boots on to go to work he just collapsed and died. I was a bit shocked, and so was the whole of the nick. They couldn't believe that Little Jack had gone so suddenly, but then the prisoners got the needle. Anger mounted. We had all had experience of casual treatment given to men who went sick. To get proper attention a man literally had to be at death's door. It seemed to us that the new set of medical officers weren't as good as the Scotsmen.

For nine years I constantly reported sick with rheumatoid arthritis. The only treatment I ever got was aspirin and some unidentifiable tablets. Not until I was crippled and bedridden and dying did the doctors finally agree that I had rheumatoid arthritis.

Meanwhile we had to do what we could for a dead mate. We knew he had no relations outside. In the ordinary course of events he would have been buried in a convict's grave in the prison grounds, but we decided to prevent that if we could. The grapevine went into operation. Word of Jack's death reached Notting Hill. We had many friends among the racing fraternity and within twenty-four hours we saw results. Georgie Cronk, the bookmaker and well-known friend of the underdog, came to Parkhurst jail by the first available boat. He took Jack's body back to Notting Hill Gate. Smothered in flowers, the handsome coffin lay in state in a turf accountant's office while burglars, ex and active, paid homage to him. His pals filed past his coffin to say their last goodbye. Among the tributes was a giant wreath from the old lags of Parkhurst. Many prisoners willingly sacrificed their tobacco to buy the wreath, but it was worth it. Wherever Jack had gone, I'll bet he was grinning happily. To be buried from a bookmaker's office would have tickled his sense of humour.

One thing you've got to have in this life is a sense of humour. My sense of humour kept me going through my life sentence and I always found something in human behaviour to amuse me.

Paddy Stewart, a lifer, was in the next cell to me. He had had a suicide pact with a girl. She lay down in front of a train and the train killed her, but he got cold feet and jumped off the line. They charged him with murder. He was convicted and reprieved. He was a strange, silent guy, a big fellow with nothing there, nothing at all, very little brain. One morning I kicked his cell door to wake him up, but he didn't come out. I thought he'd overslept. The jailer opened his door quickly and I walked past him. He was lying on the floor. He had tried to cut his cock off with a tin knife. Jack Hunt, the chief, was walking through the hall. I looked over the top of No. 5 landing. "Jack, Stewart's cut his cock off." He just laughed at me. "I'm not joking. He's smothered with blood up here." Anyway, he didn't make a very good attempt at it. He should have got a razor blade.

"God is Love" was embroidered on his tie and he was a Salvationist. He used to walk round the compound reading the Bible. After he came out of hospital and back to work in the store, I asked him, "What do you want to try and cut your cock off for?"

"Well, it's been the cause of all my trouble," he said. I thought, well, ask a silly question, etc.

The great day in Parkhurst was Cup Final Day, when A Hall played B Hall. I very rarely watched football, but I loved to see a cup final because the captain and centre-forward was a boy from Paddington called Nick Carter. He was a great fighter, afraid of no one. The A Hall team was tough and full of cockneys. In the front line was Jimmy Essex, two-time killer, left wing. Bob Hedley, convicted of murder, was right wing. Half a dozen other murderers and tearaways were in the team. They brought in an outside referee, a little short man wearing a blazer with a Hampshire badge. He gave an offside. There was a right argument. Nick chinned him and knocked him out. It was the last time we had an outside referee. The game continued, but it nearly led to a mutiny. In the other team were the Scots mob and the Northerners. What our team didn't know was that the Scots mob had had our goalie straightened. There were bets all over the place. It stank. I knew it was going to be crooked. The result? We lost 5-2.

For the first time in many years the governor gave us permission to have a concert. I wrote to the producer of one of the Ryde shows and asked him if he would bring his show in one weekend.

It was a beautiful sunny Sunday afternoon when I met them at the gate. I was wearing sunglasses, white shirt, white trousers, feeling and looking very fit. They couldn't believe I was a prisoner. We unloaded their basket of props from a shooting brake and took them up the drive to the church. There was a bit of a problem because this prison didn't cater for ladies. But I soon fixed it up with a commode from the hospital and a green screen.

The comedy was *Love in the Mist*, a very funny play. It should have been called 'Love in the Pissed', because they certainly were pissed that afternoon. My assistant stage manager was in a bit of a panic.

"What's the matter?" I asked.

"The commode is full up. What shall I do with it?"

"Well, bottle it up and sell it at fourpence a bottle. 'Maid's Water'. Plenty of sex cases in the nick for that. What do you do, you silly bastard? Throw it away."

Someone told the producer I was doing life and he asked me straight out how was it I could still laugh. Perhaps he expected me to cry all through my life sentence. Then he asked me about sex and the last time I had had a woman. I think he was a bit queer, myself. When I told him, he said, "Which one of those three would you fancy?" I thought, you must be joking, but he wasn't joking. He was serious.

"Which one?" I said. Well, they were all darlings.

"I can fix it with one of them for you. Can you manage it?"

"Can I manage it!"

There was a tunnel going through the chapel to C Hall which we'd been using as a dressing room. During the break I walked through the tunnel. Jack Hunt was too busy to notice. He was busy counting bodies going out from the first performance, and I was supposed to be getting ready for the second performance. The producer stood outside the door, but as soon as I touched her body and smelt her beautiful skin it was all over, a waste of time. Sexual intercourse, it was sexual torture. She was so beautiful—but she pitied me. That isn't the way to enjoy sex.

The second performance was much funnier than the first because some of the props, a plate of prunes and a cigarette-box with cigarettes in it, were missing. The stage assistants had nicked them. They hadn't had a prune for donkey's years.

By this time we were putting on our own shows. There was a little rat serving ten years for trading with the enemy, a conjurer by profession. The governor asked me to have him in the show. I didn't want him. He was a collaborator. He sent out for his props. His father was a big showman in the West Country, and they came in a big hamper. He was given a spare cell next door to his own to keep them in. Amongst the props were some white rabbits. There were tears in his eyes when he found his white rabbits had gone. I'm sorry to say that we had rabbit stew one night and we did enjoy it.

The great thing about these shows wasn't the performance itself but the rehearsals. One day I popped into the rehearsal room for the Christmas pantomime.

"Who's been eating my porridge?" said Father Bear.

"Who's been eating my porridge?" said Mother Bear.

Up on the stage playing the part of Little Red Riding Hood was Robbie Valentine. Father Bear had a seven-inch scar right across his face, together with a broken nose. Mother Bear was Jim the Penman, the greatest forger in England. I could hardly stop laughing. They looked a right bunch of swells up there, but this wasn't a West End rehearsal room. It was the chapel at Parkhurst jail.

I went back to work. The screw in charge of the stores was a bit of a bastard, but he had a sense of humour. I just called him Fat Joe and kept on laughing. When I told him that Scarface Nick was Father Bear, Robbie Valentine was Little Red Riding Hood, he said, "My God, they'll be giving them fairy cakes for tea next!" and for once he smiled. "Porridge, they spend half their lives in the nick eating porridge for breakfast," said Joe. I knew he had a soft spot for Robbie, a convicted murderer, a lifer who had been in jail for fourteen years, but Joe was an ex-naval P.O. and Robbie was an ex-naval officer. He was a trusted prisoner and he often used to wander into the stores, sit down and tell a tale. He had silver-grey hair, long soft hands, and was always immaculately dressed. He had all the manners of a butler and had once been yachting with Prince Philip at Cowes. He talked about boats. I felt sorry for him, fourteen years in jail. He had come home on leave from an Atlantic convoy and found his wife in bed with an air-raid warden.

"Please don't call her 'my old woman'. 'My wife', if you please."

"Sorry, Robbie," I used to say. I don't know why he insisted on 'wife', because she wasn't in circulation. He'd shot the bloody two, stone dead.

"The right thing, old boy, the right thing to do," he used to say.

"Yes," I'd say. "Quite right."

As he came past the store room one day after rehearsal, Joe

called him, "Little Red Riding Hood, come and have a cup of tea and some porridge." Forever afterwards Joe and I called him Little Red.

One day he came into our store looking downcast.

"What's troubling you, Little Red?" asked Joe.

"It's Mother Bear," said Robbie. "I've been getting that bastard Jim the Penman out of his cell every night for rehearsals. It's two days to go before Christmas and he's being released on Christmas Eve and I'll have no Mother Bear good enough by Christmas Day." This was no doubt a crisis in Little Red's life, but difficulties in jail are nearly always overcome and I had no doubt that he would produce a Mother Bear for old lags on Christmas Day. As Little Red left the store he turned and said, "When Jim the Penman comes back for his next lagging he'll never get another part in another Christmas show, I'll see to that. I'll write to the Home Secretary; the bloody bastard. Fancy going out on Christmas Eve!"

He left us raging and nearly knocked over the prison chaplain. "Hello, Padre," he said. "Just the man I want to see. It's about Mother Bear . . ."

As they disappeared along the drive, Joe said, "You'd think he was Val Parnell putting on a Command Performance at the Palladium."

Well, I enjoyed that prison concert, and so did my new pal Bobbie. Bobbie was a lifer. He'd killed a fellow during an argument, hit him over the head with a hammer. He had been sentenced to death and reprieved. The strangest thing was that he had never appealed against his death sentence. Now if someone doesn't appeal against death or try to save their own life, there must be something wrong, but he wasn't certifiable. He was quite normal. He worked well. He never petitioned to the Secretary of State and very rarely made an application to the governor. He asked for nothing and seemed to want nothing.

"Bobby, don't you want to get out of this place?" I asked him. I was determined to find out how he ticked. "Are you married?"

"Yeah," he said.

"Not divorced?"

"No."

"When's the last time you saw your wife?" I knew he received no letters from anybody.

"I haven't seen her from the night I was arrested."

"She doesn't write to you at all, does she?"

"No."

"Tell me, do you ever write to her?"

"No, how could I write to her? I wouldn't know what to say. Anyway, I think she's having an affair with some officer. She used to be in the WAAFs."

"Do you know where she lives?"

"Yeah."

"Well," I said, "what does she do?"

"She works as a vanwoman on the railway."

"Oh," I said. "Why don't you write to her?"

"No. What's the good?"

"You've got no previous convictions. You've never been in prison before. You've never been in trouble before. Why don't you try and get away from this prison to a farm or something?"

"No, when they want to let me out they'll let me out. When they want to shift me they'll shift me. I don't want nothing from them."

"Listen, Bobbie, do you love your wife?" I asked.

Reluctantly he said, "I suppose I do." Then he pulled from underneath his bed a little cardboard box. "There she is. That's Podge. That's my wife."

Oh, my God, when I looked at the picture, one of those 1930 pictures, she was ugly. "Oh, that's very nice, Bobby, very nice. Why don't you write to her? Tell you what. Let me write to her. You say you can't write a love letter. Let me write to her."

He was a bit reluctant at first, and then he agreed. I wrote and told her how much I had missed her these nine years, how I looked forward to seeing her one day, how I had always loved her, she was my first girl. I had never touched another woman. I reminded her of all these things. I wrote it on toilet paper and he copied it out and sent it off.

About a week went past and then he came into the store.

"Jim, what do you think? I got a letter from Podge." He showed it to me. It was about eighteen pages. "Read it, read it, and tell me what you think," he said.

"Look, Bobby, I've got a bit of work to do. It's eighteen pages. I'd like to analyse every sentence that's inside it. I can't do it here. I'll come over to the Association Room. I'll come over and have tea. We'll have a talk. I'll read it and work out an answer."

"Right."

Come teatime I got over there. We all had our favourite places to sit at. Bobby had tomatoes and lettuce on my plate and a bit of corned beef, like a tea party. I couldn't get through it quick enough. He was dying for me to read his letter. After the second mug of tea, I said, "Right, Bobby, give us it."

He kept interrupting me. "Now what do you think she meant by that?"

"Now leave off and let me read this letter. It's me she's writing to!"

Well, it was a passionate letter that I wrote to her, and I had to continue writing. It went on for weeks. I felt like a cheat. Then I put an idea to him. "Now you write to the Secretary of State. Let me write a petition for you."

So I wrote to the Secretary of State stating that I, Bobby . . . had never been a criminal and, having been convicted and reprieved for murder, had been in jail for nine years. I had never received a visit in nine years, but after all these years there was a possibility, in view of recent letters I had had from my wife, that if I was moved to a London jail where she could visit me, and she couldn't afford to visit me as she was working on the railway and couldn't take the time off, we could get reconciled. Could he consider transferring me to a London prison for twenty-eight days for visits?

A couple of weeks went by and funnily enough we both went away together. In London I went to Wandsworth and Robbie carried on. They took him over to Pentonville. Again I didn't see my wife and was a bit down in the dumps. (She was having an affair.) I was pleased to be going back to Parkhurst. Bobby was on the same train, smoking his pipe. His tin was full of tobacco. He was happy.

"Well, did you see her?" I asked.

"Yes."

"Did you have an open visit?"

"Oh, yes," he said. "Yeah."

"Did you kiss each other and all that?"

"Yes, of course, they let us kiss each other, yeah." He was really laughing. I had never seen him laugh before. He was happy.

"Now, that's move number one," I said. I thought it was ironic. I knew I had no chance of a reconciliation or of getting out of jail, but although I was sad for myself I was happy for

Bobby. Back at Parkhurst, I got busy with the pen again. I wrote a petition to the Secretary of State, pointing out that: I, Bobby . . . was not liable to be a menace to society. I had no criminal convictions. I had been in prison nine years. I had never been placed on report. I had a history of work. I had been reconciled to my wife, who had taken two rooms and was furnishing them. There was a home for me to go to. Would he consider releasing me?

A few weeks went by and I saw Bobby walking round what is known as 'Governor's call up'. When he came into the dining room at lunchtime he put his thumb up. The Secretary of State was going to release him. The letters continued. I now had to write out and ask her to buy me a salt-and-pepper overcoat as I was coming out in the winter. Being the storeman, one of my jobs was to receive prisoners' property. Bobby's wife sent him a plain black overcoat. He started moaning about that. I thought: "Christ! The man's going out, and he's worried what colour his overcoat is!"

The great day came, the morning for him to be released. Jack Hunt came to me.

"You'd better go down to reception. Go down and see your pal Bobby, otherwise he'll have to stay in another day."

"What's the matter?" I asked.

"He's moaning because his shoes won't fit him. He says they're too tight and he's not going out."

"Not going out? But his wife . . . I've seen her down at the gate." I'd seen Podge. She was worse than the picture. She must have weighed about eighteen stone. I went down to the cells to see him.

"What are you moaning about?" I asked.

"Look, when I come in my shoes fit me," he said. "I'm not going out with a pair of shoes like this. They're pinching my feet. I want another pair of shoes."

"You tried them on yesterday. You should have found that out yesterday. Give them to me. I'll go and get you another pair." I was very lucky. I just caught the cobbler opening up the shop. I went round and said, " 'Ere, do us a favour. Stretch these as much as you possibly can." Well, you could hear the stitches cracking. I ran back to the cells.

"Here, there's another pair. Try that pair on." He put them on.

"That's better."

"Right, you're just in time," I said, "because the screws are off for breakfast, otherwise you won't get out. Come on. Lively." I wanted to walk down to the gate with him. It's nice to see a lifer go out. I felt happy.

Bobby walked towards Podge. He didn't embrace her. He just kept looking down at his shoes, and moaning about them. He never even turned round and waved me goodbye. I was choked. I wondered if I had done the right thing and if that man would ever kill that woman.

Everyone panics when the Home Secretary comes round a jail. They put new toilet seat covers on and liven the place up. The food is always good that day. What a load of old cobblers the food-tasting racket in a jail was. It was all laid out specially. The governor tasted each dish daily. "Hmmm . . ." he said, smacking his lips as though he had just had some caviar from the Mirabelle. But I used to sweep up two or three pails of rat shit every day from the stores before delivering the flour to the bakehouse. When they complained I said it was black grain. We had tins of potatoes marked 'Not to be used after 1946'. They were still using them in 1950.

I thought I'd give the Home Secretary a pull. It was a right nicking job if you even tried to talk to him. There were only three of us in the stores, me, Robby and Paddy Stewart. The Home Secretary, Mr Chuter Ede, had been told we were lifers.

"Excuse me, sir," I said. "Can I have a word with you?" The chief's eyes nearly popped out of his head. The governor was biting his tongue.

"Yes, laddie. What can I do for you?"

"Sir, you've got the reputation of being a very fair man," I said. "I've got a little request to make. They're a bit right wing in this nick. I come out of the back streets and my parents always voted Labour. They won't let us have the *Daily Herald*, only the *Daily Telegraph* and *The Times.* We like to read the other side, the *Daily Herald*, the voice of the Labour Party, the voice of the workers."

"Is that correct, Governor?" he asked.

"Well, er . . . just, er, Commissioner's orders."

"Well, you'll have the *Daily Herald* in future, laddie."

"One other thing, sir, if you could help me," I said. "If you'll get your little book out and put my name down, I'm doing a life sentence, sir. I've been here a number of years. I've got a little bit of form, but if you start to dig into it I was no big-time criminal. I'm not liable to be a danger to society. I've got a wife and a kid and want to settle down, get to work, build up a little haulage business. I hate to say it, sir, but there's an election not far away in the future. There's always a chance that you can lose the election and if those Tories get in, I've got no chance of getting out."

He laughed. "What did you say your name was?"

"O'Connor, sir. O, apostrophe, C, O, double N, O, R, Number 437 James O'Connor, sir, aged thirty-three." I wanted to make sure he didn't forget it. He took a notebook and pencil out of his pocket and he wrote it all down.

"I'll look into it," he said. "I'll look into your case."

The weeks went by, the months went by. In the meantime I had a couple of letters. One was from Ethiopia. Archbishop Matthew, who had confirmed me in the condemned cell, sent me a copy of his latest book and told me he was sitting on the verandah with Father McMenemy, the priest on the *Lancastria*, who had become his secretary. All those miles away my name had cropped up.

Another good letter came from the Commander of the *Queens*, Harry Grattidge, the petty officer aboard the *Lancastria* when she was bombed. I had written to him asking whether he could help me, apologising for the address I was writing from and reminding him where we had last met. I thought it might be one way of getting my boy out of the back streets of Kilburn. I didn't want him to follow in my footsteps. Fortunately, he didn't. Harry Grattidge sent him to a merchant navy training school for three months and then put him on the *Queen Mary*. At different times he served on the *Queens* with George Sewell, Jnr, who later became an actor and was in several of my plays, and Tommy Steele. Eventually he joined the American Air Force in Alaska. He was a good pilot and used to fly bear shooting in the back country. Once he got nicked for landing in Canadian territory during a snowstorm, but he has never committed a real crime. He is now the superintendent of a shipping line in San Francisco, an American citizen with two beautiful children and a lovely wife. I thank the Commander of the *Queens* for that. It was the only thing I could possibly do for my son.

On October 25th, 1951, I was all at sixes and sevens. It was the day of the General Election. I thought if those Tories get in I've had it. I had the feeling that the Home Secretary knew they were going to get in. In my layman's opinion the Labour Party had had it. I thought he might just let me out before he leaves. He might.

The following morning was Saturday. They were out. The Tories were in. I felt a bit despondent. I had just picked up a sack of sugar to take round to the kitchen when a jailer called me.

"O'Connor, the governor wants you, urgent."

I don't know why, but I had an intuition. I thought it could be, it could be my son, it could be.

I walked into the governor's office. There he was, sitting at a desk, holding a paper.

"I have to inform you that the Secretary of State has ordered you to be released on March 15th, 1952," he said formally.

I felt as though someone had thrown a bucket of cold water over me.

"Cor, strike me blind," I said, and crossed myself; not very dramatic, but I just felt a terrific shock. "That's a bit of a liberty," I said.

"Aren't you happy going out?"

"Yes, of course I'm happy," I said. "But every other lifer gets three weeks or four weeks. Why sort me out? Five months I've got to wait. March 15th."

I walked out of the room in a daze. Naturally I was glad, but I wished they had not told me so far in advance. I knew those last five months were going to be like five stretch. And suppose something stopped me getting out after all?

I went back to the store, sat down on a sack of sugar and put a cigarette in my mouth. The old storeman looked at me and said, "You've gone quiet all of a sudden. What's the matter?"

"Well, as a matter of fact, mate, I've been knocked a bit sick. I am going out."

"You're kidding."

"No," I said, "I'm not kidding."

"Well, I'm glad to hear that," he said. "Sit down there, have a cup of tea."

I was a bit worried about Robbie, the other lifer in the stores. He said nothing and kept looking at me queerly. Robbie had already done fifteen stretch. Although he said nothing, I knew he couldn't help resenting the fact that I was getting out after only ten years and ten months. I understood his feelings. It would have been just the way I would have felt if I had been in his shoes.

I went back to my cell and after I had had my dinner lay down on my bed. There were letters to write to my mother, my son and other relatives. Somehow I had to arrange for some money. All I would get from the prison authorities would be five shillings and a letter to the National Assistance or the Prisoners After Care at Eccleston Square, and I couldn't live long on that.

I woke just before two o'clock with the screw's keys jangling and heavy footsteps coming along the passage. I went to reach for a cigarette and a lighter lying on my chair by my bed, but I found I couldn't move my arms. The door burst open. News travels round the jail very fast. In came half a dozen screws and a couple of prisoners. The cell was full. "Good luck, Ginger boy", "Heard the good news", from both sides.

"Yes," I said, then I started to laugh. "Listen, I can't move."

"You're joking."

"I tell you I can't move. Do me a favour. Light me a cigarette."

"Come on, get off that bed. You'll be in the boozer in a few weeks' time; then in bed with a bird."

"I don't want to be in bed with no birds. I'm telling you I can't move." I could move my head. It was the only part of my body I could move. Someone lit a cigarette for me and I was taken over to the hospital on a stretcher. I couldn't walk. I was paralysed from the neck down. My wrists and knees were swollen like cricket balls. They put me in a cell, not an open ward, which suited me fine. The way I was feeling I didn't want company. My condition grew steadily worse. I couldn't move my hands and feet and was completely helpless. A specialist came from London especially to examine me. They took samples of fluid from my swollen knee, gave me tablets, belladonna, gold injections and then they nearly killed me with bee injections. Instead of ten thousand units, Nobby gave me a hundred thousand units. Mind you, Nobby was a bit short-sighted. I woke up at half past three in the morning and found the priest beside me.

"What are you doing, Father?"

"I was called in to give you the last rites. It was touch and go, boy, touch and go."

The following morning I had a relapse and they brought the priest in again. But I got better slowly. The Slug paid a visit to my cell. The others used to leave my door open, but he couldn't shut it quick enough. Day after day I willed myself to get my limbs moving. In the middle of the night I used to force myself to try and straighten out. I began to move my fingers up the wall and at last the paralysis began to heal. Towards the end of December I began to get back the use of my hands and my arms. A good old lag used to carry me to the loo. I walked round the landing with my hands on his hips and gradually got on to his shoulders, then on to sticks. By Christmas I was walking for a few minutes a day.

In February 1952 I was transferred from Parkhurst to Wormwood Scrubs to be seen by specialists at Hammersmith Hospital, next door to the jail. It wasn't far to the hospital, not more than a ten-minute walk, but we always had to use a car. I enjoyed those short car journeys. Looking out of the window, I used to think in a couple of weeks I'll be walking those streets a free man.

In Wormwood Scrubs I met a prisoner called Alec Crawford, a brother of Jack Crawford who had helped me fight my case. I told him I was grateful to his brother for helping me, and he explained that his brother had only helped me because he knew who had committed the murder. He told me that the man was one of three brothers, one of whom used to work for him. He said that I knew the murderer, but that he was terrified of getting into trouble and wouldn't tell me the man's name until he was released. He told me to go and see his brother Jack who had a pub and would tell me all that he and his family knew. Another brother in Willesden would let me have a lorry to set me up for work.

The night before my release I kept imagining seeing my boy at the gate next morning. I had waited years to see him. I thought I wouldn't sleep that night, but I did. I slept like a log. I thought that after all those years in jail I would be awake like a greyhound coming out of his trap. The night watchman couldn't make it out. He had to keep banging on my door. The old boy was happy to see me going out. He was a local man from Notting Hill Gate.

In my civvy clothes I went over to the chief prison officer's office by the main gates, where I had to sign for my licence, my lifer's licence. This says that the Secretary of State can recall me at any time he thinks fit, but typed on a piece of paper stuck to it was a note saying that I was not to worry about this. I would only be recalled for crimes of violence.

11

"I'm warning you Ginger. Drop it or . . . ."

Out on the pavement my mother and a few friends were waiting with a car. To my disappointment I couldn't see my son. I didn't expect to see my wife. My mother was smiling and crying at the same time. A friend who had been in France with me, Jimmy O'Donnell, was also there with Tom Tullet of the *Sunday Express.* I thought Jimmy had come to see me as a pal. They drove me to my mother's in Maida Vale. She had saved up and bought a bottle of scotch to celebrate.

Over the drinks Tullet promised me all sorts of things about selling my life story. And he got what he wanted, his front page lead. In those days I didn't even understand the expression. Then he pissed off. I never got a penny.

After Tullet had left, I went with my mother and her friend Ted to see an old friend of mine, a publican who ran the Dudley Arms facing Paddington Green Police Station and who used to visit me at Dartmoor. As soon as I arrived Freddie took me into his office, opened his safe, gave me a hundred quid and told me he was going to set me up in a little business, but that first of all I was to have a few days' rest. He rang Jack Crawford, who told me to come over and see him on Monday at his pub, The Northern Star, at Southgate.

The pub was virtually empty except for Jimmy O'Donnell, my mother, Freddie and his wife. I went upstairs to Freddie's private apartment, where he told me to choose any clothes I wanted until I got myself measured up at his tailors down to him. He was that kind of guy and would always help the underdog, although he was never a receiver or crooked and worked hard all his life. He knew that I was innocent.

When I came down from Freddie's flat there was one solitary customer sitting in the corner of the pub. I looked at him. His face seemed familiar to me. It was quite a long bar. I looked at my friends and at my mother. They knew and I didn't. I was just about to move towards him to ask him when Jimmy O'Donnell got hold of my arm. He was as strong as a lion. In actual fact, I couldn't have done much because I was weak and had lost a lot of weight. Then the man got up and left the pub.

"Is that man's name Arthur Goodman?" I asked.

"We don't know, but he often comes in here," they said.

"Oh, yes," I said. "I thought it was." The man was my wife's lover. I asked them if they'd all excuse me and let me go. I wanted to walk alone and walk along the pavements. They understood. It was nice to walk along the streets. I was nervous of the traffic when walking across the road. I went into a pub called The Chippenham near where I was brought up as a kid and a couple of hundred yards from the scene of the murder. I was looking. I don't know what I was looking for, but I was looking.

I was thinking about my son. I wanted to see him. I knew he had finished his course at the Mercantile Naval Training College, and was working at the Grosvenor Hotel as a page boy, following his father's footsteps while he was waiting for a boat. Harry Grattidge wanted to get him on the *Queen Mary.*

Two local C.I.D. men walked into the pub. News travels fast. Someone had been on the blower.

"Just a minute, Jimmy boy. We'd like to have a word with you."

"Well, give us a chance. I've only just come out. What do you want me for?"

"The guv'nor wants to see you."

"The guv'nor? What for?"

"He's outside in the car. Come out. Do yourself a favour."

I went outside. I didn't know the guv'nor.

"Hello, son," he said. "Just a little word of warning to you. Do yourself a favour. We know you've only just come out this morning, but don't go near your wife or her boyfriend. They've been to see us. They came yesterday, complained that you were coming out."

My wife was drawing a pension while I was in jail which ended as soon as I came out. But she had been hoping she would be able to draw it for a few more years. I didn't blame her, but did she want to keep me in for ever? Especially as I was actually with her when the murder was committed.

"Don't worry about that, guv'nor," I said. "I just want to see my son."

In the late afternoon I arrived at my wife's home and went in. The man from Freddie's pub was there, sitting in my armchair and surrounded by about fifteen of his pals. I looked at them. They were what we call half wide mugs. You couldn't have a straight argument or fight with people like them. They would blow the whistle and thanks. By warning the coppers they had marked my card. I asked them where my son was. They said he was working at the Grosvenor and didn't finish till midnight.

Someone told an old school pal of mine that I was in the house. He rushed in with his brother and took me away from those people. They took me to a pub and gave me a few quid. Everywhere I went people were putting money into my pockets. I stopped drinking. I knew I couldn't take it, and went home to my mother's. There was a made-up bed for me in the kitchen. Nice, I thought. I had a better bed in the nick. I come out. Someone's nicked my wife and my home. I tried to go to sleep. There was a party taking place for me. I locked myself in the kitchen, but I couldn't sleep.

I walked along the Edgware Road into the West End. At dawn I found myself walking beside the Thames, then up Whitehall and into Scotland Yard, where I asked to see a Superintendent I knew. My case was bugging me. My wife was bugging me. The Superintendent wasn't on duty. A jovial Sergeant at the door asked me my name.

"Oh, I've just been reading about you in the paper," he said. "Just a minute, son." He picked up the phone. The C.I.D. came up to see me and took me down to the canteen.

"What's the trouble? Can we help you?"

"Listen, if you went home and found someone indoors with your old woman, what would you do?" I said.

One of the coppers said, "I'd sling the bastard out."

"Why can't I do it?" I said. "Why can't I do it without getting nicked?"

"Ah, it's not worth it, son," they said. "Get yourself into trouble for nothing. Forget all about it."

"Well, I want to go there to see my son. That's all."

"There's nothing to stop you from doing that," they said. "But don't have a row with anybody and take a witness."

I walked up towards Piccadilly, and in the newspapers lying outside Lyons Corner House I saw pictures of myself walking out of the gates at the Scrubs and Tom Tullet's story headlined: "I CAN PROVE I DID NOT COMMIT MURDER".

I called a cabby. He was a Yiddisher cabby.

"Listen, I want you to do me a favour. Take me to Kilburn." I gave him a fiver. "If you've got plenty of time to spare there'll be a bit more for you before the day's out."

I arrived at my wife's. The cabby came with me. I knocked on the door. My wife and her lover opened it. Early in the morning, they were fully dressed. They had been sitting up all night, waiting.

I looked at the geezer. I call him that. It was just what he looked like. I looked at his face and said to him:

"Tell me, do you love my wife?"

He sort of muttered.

I asked her: "Do you love this fellow?" She couldn't even answer. "Well, he wants to know even if I don't."

"I don't know," she said.

"Well, make up your mind. Anyway, where's my son?"

"He's asleep."

"Well, wake him up. I'd like to see him." I sat and looked at them. My boy came out of the passage.

I asked him, "Son, tell me, what do you call him?"

"Uncle Arthur."

"You know who I am, don't you?"

"Yes, you're my dad."

"Tell me, who do you want to be with? Me or him?"

"Uncle Arthur," he said.

"That's all right, son. I understand."

I walked away. "Take your clothes off, go to bed, go to sleep," I said. "Forget all about me. Goodbye and good luck."

When I got back to the cab the cab driver had been reading the papers that I had left. Naturally, I had bought them all; vanity, I wanted to read about myself.

"Take me to that block of council flats down there." He took me down. I went to see my pal Bill. I knocked on the door. A little boy opened it. By this time Bill had six kids.

"Is your dad in? Bill, is he in?"

"Hello there, who's that?"

"It's me." I walked into his bedroom. We shook hands. He got out of bed, got dressed. His wife cooked me some breakfast and then we went to a pub and had a couple of drinks.

At half past three on Sunday afternoon a *Daily Mail* reporter called at my mother's. He said he wanted to help me prove I was innocent. I told him that I was going to see Jack Crawford on Monday. He asked me a few questions. The *Daily Mail* published the story. Jack Crawford clammed up. He was very annoyed about the *Daily Mail* story. He wouldn't tell me the name of the murderer and said that he was afraid of him. "He's killed once before, you know." He gave me a cheque for fifty pounds.

My case was still bugging me. Mrs Van der Elst, a great campaigner for abolition of the death penalty, contacted me and offered to help.

On Thursday morning I went to Scotland Yard and saw Chief Inspector Thorp. I accused him of framing me and demanded to see the watch and chain. He told me this had been returned to the jeweller in Bath city and sent for the property book to show me the signature of a Mr Littuar, the jeweller, as having received the watch and chain from Scotland Yard. He advised me to forget it.

A private detective retained by Mrs Van der Elst interviewed George Sewell, who admitted that he had been given the watch and chain, used by the prosecution as the main evidence against me at my trial, well before the murder.

A firm of solicitors in Bath acting for Mrs Van der Elst told me that the jeweller was prepared to inspect the watch and chain. I was amazed because I had been shown his signature for the receipt of the watch and chain at Scotland Yard. I telephoned Thorp and accused him of forging Mr Littuar's signature.

In April 1952 I visited the house where George Ambridge was murdered. While I was standing outside, a woman I knew came up to me and said she thought a girl called Florence Sayers had something to do with the murder. She told me that when Flo Sayers was broke she used to sleep with George Ambridge. He wasn't so old, after all. Her husband had been in prison for living on immoral earnings and she lived with convicted criminals. When one went to jail she changed to another. Flo

Sayers was a friend of my wife's and in one of my petitions I found that I had mentioned her name in a small sentence. On the night of the murder I had said good night to her as she was walking home with a man she was living with in Kilburn. Whilst I was in Dartmoor she died and I read in the *Kilburn Times* that she had been buried in a pauper's grave.

The People newspaper took up my case and with Duncan Webb, their top crime reporter at the time, I traced Mr Littuar, the jeweller in Bath. He had a Van Dyke beard and was in his dressing-gown. He gave us drinks while he finished his breakfast. Then he told Duncan Webb that he had never been to Scotland Yard in his life or signed a property book for receiving a watch and chain, and that he had never heard of Superintendent Nat Thorp. If there was a signature in the book it was a forgery. I told him that my father had sent me a telegram to Dartmoor on 2nd September 1942, following a telephone call he had had from a detective at Scotland Yard telling him that the watch and chain had been identified as having been stolen from Bath.

The *Sunday Dispatch* published a story about me and as a result George Ambridge's brother wrote to Christen Peterson, the Editor, saying, "My brother never owned a gold watch and chain. The only watch and chain is the one that I am enclosing for you." It was a silver watch and chain found on George Ambridge's body when he was discovered murdered.

The Editor gave it to me.

In April I went to live with a girl in Paddington. Living facing me was a petty thief, one of three brothers, whom I shall call Mr A.

The first time I saw him after I moved in I said hello, but he ignored me. I let it pass and thought maybe after eleven years in jail he didn't recognise me. I knew that he had once been charged with killing and acquitted. He had a friend named Ernest Thomas.

During the investigation into my case I met a man called Jack Fishman, News Editor and Deputy Editor of the *Sunday Empire News*. On the basis of the facts and the new evidence from Bath he agreed to support my fight and published the story on the front page of the paper at the beginning of May. A few days later I went to see Jack Fishman, as I had had a message from Thorp at Scotland Yard asking me to telephone him. I was nervous, as I was certain he had contacted me because of the publicity about my case in the newspapers. Jack Fishman suggested that I make the call from his office. He dialled the number and asked for Thorp's extension. Then he listened on the extension phone. Afterwards Jack Fishman made a sworn statement (and to the police) and repeated the final part of the conversation.

> "O'Connor suddenly said, 'You know I'm innocent and I'm going to keep on till I prove I didn't do it.' Thorp's reply was, 'I'm warning you, Ginger. Drop it or I'll put it on you again like I did last time and next time it will be for the rest of your life.' Thorp then hung up."

After this conversation I attended a counsel's conference organised by the solicitors in Bath city who were acting for Mrs Van der Elst. There were about twelve people in the room just near the law courts in the Strand when I told them that I had been threatened by Superintendent Thorp and that I was going to drop the case because I was a cockney and 'A nod's as good as a wink', as we say. I was ashamed that I was letting these people down, but the fear of being framed by the police was deeply embedded in me. I have known many people who have been framed. A man in Thorp's position could just tell one of his subordinates to nick me and I would have been nicked after only a few weeks of liberty. I decided that I would wait. It was a campaign which needed money and time to research and dig up the evidence, and I was prepared to do this. I used to find myself like a wet house rag continually, waking up in the morning and thinking about my case, but I knew that one day Thorp would retire.

In the meantime I needed to work. I became a crime reporter for Jack Fishman on the *Sunday Empire News.* I negotiated series, thought of ideas and sold them. Most of these were involved with crime, but that is what I knew best. Doors were opened to me all over the place and I used to get first-hand information. One of Jack's crime reporters had the dead needle with me. He used to dash in on the Friday or Saturday night with an exclusive crime story and Jack would just look up and say, "I've got it. Jimmy did the story on Tuesday."

I used to get a Number 18 bus from the Harrow Road to Gray's Inn Road and the Kemsley House Building. One morning as I was leaving the house in Paddington I saw Mr A's furniture being moved into a van. Again he did not want to speak to me. I talked about him to the girl I was living with and she told me that he had lived there with a girl for nine years and before that with Flo Sayers near George Ambridge's Kilburn house at the time of the murder.

In fact, he was the man with Flo Sayers who my wife and I had passed on the night of George Ambridge's murder. I wondered why he was moving. It was pure coincidence that I had taken a room near by. If he had said 'Hello' to me I would never have discussed him.

Since my release many people have helped me. As a journalist I built up many contacts and began to see how the social system worked; the hypocrisy of so-called respectable society, the graft and corruption of property dealers, the milking of pension funds, the way hire-purchase operated, and the buying and selling of public companies to make private fortunes. This all came over a period of time, but when I first became a journalist I was absolutely amazed to discover the number of people who were on the secret pay roll of newspapers. I just kept my mouth shut and placed them in a category and left them there.

One man who helped me and would always lend me a few hundred pounds if I was broke was Paddy Kennedy, the publican at The Star Tavern in Belgrave Square. Through him I met the Mayfair and Belgravia set. He took me everywhere and I was accepted. With my cockney vernacular and my cockney jokes I was a novelty at that time. I was well dressed and I think I could go anywhere.

And so I lived in two worlds. As a journalist I had to live in all worlds. I used to go to a pub off the Portobello Road used by criminals, some active, some reformed, some retired, and barrow boys. It was run by an old lag from Dartmoor.

I started to fight the Establishment and exposed all kinds of miscarriages of justice, brutalities in jail, and innocent people. I became interested in everybody. I wanted to know, I had to know, but I learned to keep my mouth shut. I divorced my wife. I was a bachelor and free to do whatever I liked and go wherever I liked.

I used to go to a club in South Audley Street in Mayfair. A jeweller called Mr Addy was often there with his wife. They had a little black poodle who used to wag his tail, and they often sent me across drinks. One day he asked me why I looked so sad and always sat alone. I told them I wasn't sad, but I sat alone because I was thinking. They invited me to dinner and said they had some business they would like to talk to me about. They were well spoken and well dressed, and we went to a restaurant in Sloane Avenue. Then they put a proposition to me about robbing a jeweller in Hatton Garden. I realised that these people didn't know I was a journalist and not a criminal. To them I was a murderer. I think I shocked them a bit. I couldn't waste my time. I left.

It is strange when people look upon you as a murderer. On another occasion I was sitting with a tycoon in his car in Belgrave Square when he pushed a black wallet towards me.

"Inside there is five thousand pounds. In this package is a syringe. Now I want you to inject that in the pubic hairs of Mr X. There will be no trace of it."

I looked at him and thought there's a right nutter here, but I knew his history. He wasn't a nutter. He was a very clever man.

"What is the matter with you?" I asked him.

"This man's having an affair with my wife."

"Number one I am not a killer, and number two if someone's upset domestic life between you and your wife you won't achieve anything by killing anybody." I pushed the money back to him and we went and had a drink. When he told me the man's name I told him how to beat his wife's lover. He did, and he and his wife were reconciled.

Another time a journalist asked me if I could look after a woman called Betty Jones for a week, whose life story he was ghosting. She was a convicted murderer. Her accomplice, an American serviceman, was hanged. They had killed a taxi driver. She lived in Acacia Avenue, Hampstead. I was in her flat one day when she said, "Wouldn't it be a good idea if you and I were to get married?"

"Married? I don't want to get married!"

"Well, you know, two murderers marrying each other. It would make a marvellous story."

I went on my first journalistic mission abroad. The Russians were releasing a British prisoner and handing him over to the British in Hanover. The name published in the newspapers was the wrong one, but eventually I traced his mother and brother.

I went and saw Mrs Kelly, spoke to her in her language and gave her a nice few quid from my pocket. I asked her if she'd like to speak to her son on the telephone. She called him 'Bunny'. It was his nickname. My job was to get Private Kelly signed up for the *Empire News.* The following week a press conference was arranged for him, but I managed to lobby a Member of Parliament and stop that, and the rest of the press hadn't found Mrs Kelly.

I went to sleep that night, but woke up at four in the morning. I had the feeling there was something wrong. I didn't know what. I drove across to South London and waited for the light to come on and the smoke to come out of the chimney. At five o'clock I went into the house to ask Mrs Kelly if anyone else had been to see her since my last visit. She looked a bit nervous.

"What's the matter, darling? Come and tell me. There's something on your mind."

"Well, there's a man been here who told me I'm not to talk to you. You've been in prison for murder," she said.

"What man?"

"Duncan Webb of *The People*. He said you're not a journalist."

"Mrs Kelly, can I ask you one question? Did he give you any money?"

"No," she said.

"Did I give you any money?"

"Yes."

"Did I ask you to sign anything, make any promises?"

"No."

"When's he going to come and see you again?"

"He's coming this morning at ten o'clock."

Well, I had her out of the house by six o'clock in the morning. By nine o'clock we were in the passport office and then I took her into the Army and Navy Stores to buy some clothes. That was when I discovered she still had her pyjamas on. By eleven o'clock we were on a plane for Hanover.

At the hotel we were met by Anthony Terry, then the political correspondent for Kemsley, and Ian Fleming. Private Kelly had been handed over to the British in Hanover and was in hospital under strict security. The only person allowed into the hospital was Kelly's mother. I used to take her there every day and hand her over at the gate. Under no condition was she to go out except to see her son. The world's press was there and all types of people offered me money. On one occasion I even had to keep Mrs Kelly locked in the bathroom so as not to let the press near her.

I had a long chat with Ian Fleming. He told me that I had lots of good ideas.

"If I were you, laddie, I'd cash in on them now, because you'll find in another two years' time you'll run out of them."

I decided to apply a bit of British psychology to get into that security block. All wars and crimes stop on Saturday midday. The way I see it, that is the British mentality. It's like Parliament. When they go into recess it's the hardest thing in the world to get them back, no matter what the crisis.

I chose Saturday afternoon, when there was a shortage of staff, to go up the fire escape. I climbed in through the window and hid under the bed. I apologised for my entrance and told him not to get upset. His mother had apparently told him how good I had been to her. I asked him if he could quickly tell me who he was in prison with, and he mentioned Cardinal Mindszenty, said he'd nursed him. I asked him if I could buy him anything. He said he'd like a set of chess. He told me he had spent most of his time in solitary in the Russian prison, and I wondered how he'd learnt to play chess. He was very reticent, and the more questions I asked, the more I felt there was something missing. I told him he had to trust me and that if he went before the world's press he had no story to sell, but if he wanted to start life afresh with a few thousand pounds in his pocket, he just had to sign this piece of paper. While I was talking to him from under the bed, the brass entered. Two guards were outside. After they left I knew I was making him very nervous. I put the pen in his hand and he signed it.

I beat the world's press to that one. I took Mrs Kelly out. She was so happy. She had never made a plane trip before, she had never been to a nightclub before, and her 'Bunny' was coming home. On his release in England, Private Kelly gave me his Russian prison uniform with a fur hat and a rough twill fur-lined prison jacket. It was the last present I wanted.

My old pal Nobby was transferred from Dartmoor to Wakefield. He had taken some good advice, 'Always get yourself a stoker's job'. I was pleased that Nobby had finished up as a stoker, and I was also pleased for another reason that he was in Wakefield. Two gentlemen I was interested in were also there.

Going to the Isle of Wight a few years earlier I had been handcuffed to one, Alan Nunn-May, the atomic spy, and the other was Klaus Fuchs, who was serving fourteen years for espionage.

In Wakefield I stayed in a jailer's house. Dr Klaus Fuchs was writing a thesis on Jesus Christ and I managed to get hold of his notebooks from his cell, photostat them and put them back the same day. The middleman between myself and Fuchs was Nobby. When the jailer came home one night after duty and gave me an envelope I could have fallen through the ceiling. The note inside was signed by Donald Hume. He had taken the place of Nobby, who had gone sick. Donald Hume was serving a twelve-year sentence for the manslaughter of a car dealer, Max Setty. He was an informer. It was a dangerous situation for Nobby and I because in those days we could have been nicked under the Official Secrets Act. I had already sold this story to *Time* and *Life* as well as the *Empire News*. I knew I had to kid Hume, so I had an idea for a series, "I got away with murder". I only had to explain to him that he could not be tried a second time, that he would get a nice few thousand pounds, and I had sold the story. He agreed to everything I said. I sent him some money. I was mainly concerned about my friend Nobby because I knew this man had us by the cobblers if he opened his mouth. But he never did.

I had given one of my first plays to Fabian of the Yard and had a message that he wanted to see me about it. I left the office and went across to Barney Finnegan's pub.

Bob Fabian was there with his jovial smile.

"What are you drinking, Jimmy?"

Standing with him was a little guy wearing a green pork-pie hat, stocky and tough. Bob asked me if I would like to have some lunch with him and his friend.

"Who's your friend?" I said.

"This is—er—Albert Pierrepoint."

He was the last person I wanted to meet. He shook hands with me. It was like the handshake of death. I put the drink which Bob had just bought me back on the counter. Pierrepoint was looking me up and down. I felt as though he was eyeing me up for the drop. No doubt Bob had marked his card and told him all about me, that I had been reprieved. It was ironic I had to meet him. To be quite honest, I didn't feel too good on meeting him. I made some excuse and said that I had to meet someone. Then Bob told me that he had fixed up for me to see the B.B.C. about my play the following day.

The B.B.C. told me they thought my play was very good, but all that they wanted to buy from me was the dialogue. I met the producer and dictated a script to her. It was one of the first semi-documentaries ever done by the B.B.C. in the mid-fifties. I sat in on the casting and helped to choose the actors.

The B.B.C. said that to get permission to film inside a jail they would have to take my name off the script. I understood that. I didn't want to stop them getting the real McCoy. Building a set in the studio is no substitute for the real thing. My name was taken off the script and they were given permission. That didn't hurt me. I was asked to attend rehearsals, and what did hurt me was that the day I arrived apparently Governor Lawton was turning up, and within three minutes of arriving I was asked to leave because he was coming. I slunk out of that building with my tail between my legs. I thought, fuck the B.B.C. They paid me a large sum of money, fifteen guineas. *Beyond the Gate* was very successful. My name was not on it. I dictated it word for word.

I saw Bob Fabian again in Barney Finnegan's and thanked him for trying to help me. I told him what the B.B.C. had done to me. He was a bit annoyed, but there was nothing much he could do about it. It took me another ten years to break into television script writing. I wanted to get away from journalism. It made me sick.

12

"They had to strap him to a board before they could top him"

Barney took a new pub in Fetter Lane. We were all there for the opening, and who else turned up? Albert Pierrepoint. Barney Finnegan was a great character and I wondered what the relationship was between him and Albert Pierrepoint. On the front of a Christmas card from Albert to Barney was the wording, "Help the Poor Struggler", which was the name of Albert Pierrepoint's pub. The drawing was a drunk hanging from an old-fashioned lamp-post by his braces. I thought that was a bit strong and realised that he loved publicity.

I discovered that he and Barney had been pals for years and every time he came down to London to hang someone he stayed in Barney's pub. The following day, on the eve of the execution, he had to be at the prison with his assistant not later than four p.m.

At about half past eleven one morning I went down to Barney Finnegan's pub to change a cheque. While I was in the private side entrance leading to Barney's apartment I saw Albert Pierrepoint with a beautiful black eye. I knew that morning he had just hanged a guardsman for a murder at Purley. I thought, hello, there's a good story here. I rang the newsroom.

"Send me down a photographer."

I wanted to snatch a picture of Pierrepoint coming out of Barney's pub. I thought this would contribute towards the abolition of the death penalty.

"There's a battle royal taken place here this morning. The guardsman's had a go."

I telephoned a senior chaplain in the prison service. I traced him to a place in Dorset. He had gone on sick leave.

"Jimmy, I don't want to talk about it," he said.

"You mean you can't talk about it. Tell me, was it as bad as all that?"

"It was as bad as all that. There was a blood bath took place. He fought for his life, the guardsman. They had to strap him to a board before they could top him."

The news room didn't send me down a photographer.

"We can't, Jimmy."

"I don't understand it. Why not? There's a marvellous story."

"We can't," they said. "He's a lot of help to us."

Pierrepoint was given a lot of money for his life story. I was to fill in with certain people he had executed. Although it would have meant a couple of thousand pounds for me, I didn't want it and turned the job down.

But I did have the pleasure of reading all his personal private notes. When he was a little boy riding on the back of a cart down a country lane he heard his father, who had been an executioner for twenty years, and his uncle, who had been an executioner for forty years, discussing different techniques of hanging. It was then that he decided he would follow in his father's footsteps. Albert Pierrepoint was Britain's hangman for twenty-five years and now says he's against it. It solves nothing and is a form of barbarism. Well, we all know that. He's a bit late. Those who want the return of hanging ought to be made to stay in a jail on the eve of an execution or be asked to witness one. I am sure they would have a change of heart. It took him a long time to change his heart.

I had an intense personal dislike for Albert Pierrepoint, not as an individual, but as a hangman. It had nothing to do with my own case, but with a girl who I used to know called Ruth Ellis. I used to drink with her and the man she killed in a club in Knightsbridge. I worked hard on the Ruth Ellis story and did as much as I possibly could to save her life. I didn't want any payment.

But Ruth did have one good friend, a girl who worked as a waitress at Bolsom's restaurant in Mayfair. She was not mercenary. Her main concern was what was going to happen to Ruth Ellis's two children. We bought her story and had the money paid to the two children.

I had a little contact in Notting Hill Gate. One day he telephoned and told me he had something interesting to tell me. He had been with a couple of birds in a club and was now back at their flat. After about ten minutes I realised that one of them was a whore. Every Friday night she had a client who came and stayed the night with her, but the previous night this man had left early. He had telephoned a hotel somewhere in Surrey and booked in and told her he wasn't going to stay the night with her. He said that no doubt the police would be looking for him because he had given Ruth Ellis the gun and driven her to Hampstead where she killed her lover. I immediately telephoned the newsroom from a phone in the flat. They told me not to leave the girl. I tried to find out from her the name of her client, but she didn't know it. All she knew was that he came every Friday. I asked her where he had made the phone call from to the hotel. At the time she was messing about in the flat and hadn't taken much notice. I picked up the pad at the side of the phone. There was no writing on it, but there were some indentations. The newspaper sent a despatch rider over to me and by enlarging it they discovered the name of a hotel and the phone number.

A reporter was sent to the hotel, but he still did not know the man's name. Unfortunately the reporter was a heavy drinker. He asked the manager if any man had booked into the hotel the night before. There was one and only one, and he had naturally gone under a false name. Having found this out, the reporter naturally made for the bar.

When the man came back to the hotel the manager told him that a reporter was looking for him and he was in the bar. He had been so pissed that he had not only told the manager his name, but also the paper he worked for. Needless to say, the character, whether he gave Ruth Ellis that gun or not, left the hotel that night.

Pierrepoint retired in 1956. Warwick Charlton, a very good journalist, and I decided to go up to his home and interview him. I disguised myself as much as possible, wearing thick glasses and with my hair cut short. Just outside Manchester it was pouring down with heavy rain when we went into the local pub at lunchtime, a great big pub, soulless and empty. We asked about the home of Mr Pierrepoint. Warwick was a well-educated, well-spoken, typical English type.

"Yes, it's the house along on the right with the green roof," said the publican.

There was no reply at the house on the right with the green

roof. Maybe she's out shopping, we thought. We let the hired car go and went to the local cinema to see a Marilyn Monroe film.

When we came out we went to the house and rang the bell. Mrs Pierrepoint opened the door. Warwick could put some down. I kept my mouth closed. She invited us in to what we cockneys call the front room. It was a soulless room, just ice cold. There wasn't an ashtray in it. She gave us a cup of tea. I was afraid to light a cigarette. I just wanted to listen. She looked such a nice person with whitish-grey hair and a red and healthy complexion. I thought, I wonder how this woman feels living with a killer, because to me that is just what Albert was.

Anyway, Warwick put the story down that we were doing a thing on Alexander and Lord Montgomery and people who had retired, a lot of old nonsense we gave people when we wanted to get into them. She told us that every Wednesday night he went to a pub the other side of Manchester where he met some friends. She told us the name of the pub, and Warwick, the photographer and I took the train to Manchester and went there. We gave the publican the story that we were doing an article on Manchester, the historical monuments and ancient buildings and we had discovered that this pub was very old. Had he any objections if we took photographs of some of the customers sitting around? We bought all the old girls and everybody in the pub a drink and put that down to expenses. There was only one problem. Would Albert Pierrepoint recognise me? Warwick didn't know him. I was playing darts when Albert came in.

"That's him," I said.

But we had a surprise waiting for us. He lifted up the flap of the bar and went into a private room which we had already seen half a dozen enter.

There was a marble fireplace and above the fireplace was a picture of the guv'nor of the pub, his wife and one of the councillors of Manchester city and Albert Pierrepoint. After a time Warwick did his usual party piece.

"Excuse me, sir, I understand that that's Albert Pierrepoint. I wonder if we could have a word with him."

"Well, it's a bit difficult because he's in conference with his friends," he said.

We didn't know it, but this was a meeting point, a room of

death, where young assistants and deputies sat down to discuss the techniques and methods of hanging.

At closing time we asked the guv'nor whether he'd like to join us in a bottle of champagne. He agreed. We lifted up the flap and went behind the counter.

I sat casually down between the councillor and Pierrepoint. The councillor asked me what I did and I told him I was a writer and worked for various magazines and newspapers. Warwick quickly saved the situation and mentioned the ancient monuments of Manchester.

The missus of the pub was a bit flirty. A few smutty jokes were being thrown about and we kept ordering the booze. I looked at some of the young men, potential executioners, and thought for God's sake, Warwick, let's get what we want and get out of this pub.

"Mr Pierrepoint, they tell me you were a very sick man," I said. "You look very strong to me. I'll do you the arm game." I started doing the arm game. He was quite strong, but I done him.

Warwick gave him the retirement story.

"Well, no one's interested in me now because, you know, I haven't hanged anybody for years," said Pierrepoint.

Warwick pointed out that this was a lot of nonsense. Of course people were interested in anybody who carried out any kind of a public duty. Yes, he agreed to all that.

By this time we knew our photographer had got all the pictures he wanted. I put the question to him:

"Tell me, sir, has your conscience ever troubled you since you hung Ruth Ellis?"

He went quiet over this and then said, "I don't want to talk about that."

I was outside Holloway jail the morning they hanged Ruth Ellis, hoping that something might happen at the last minute. I had spoken to Dr Mathison, who had seen her in the condemned cell. He himself had broken down and cried. Outside was McIver of the Yard. I just looked at him. He knew me. We knew each other from Paddington. I couldn't speak to him. Mrs Van der Elst, the abolitionist, was there, screaming. I didn't even want to talk to her. I didn't want to talk to anybody. When it was all over and she was gone, the crowds still hung around. I went off and got pissed. I felt unclean because I myself had been standing outside that jail while they were hanging that woman. I felt that I was partly responsible because I couldn't find the man who gave her the gun.

That night I finished up at Churchill's Club dancing with a little girl. For me to dance I must have been pissed. Who was dancing with a darling? Jim the Penman, Mother Bear from the Moor. As I passed him I whispered, "Who's been eating my porridge?" His bow tie nearly popped.

I asked him about Little Red and was shocked to learn that after fifteen years on the Moor, Little Red was working in the mailbag shop. He had lost all his privileges and job of trust because he had tried to escape. Little Red was apparently heart-broken, a different man. After fifteen years without breaking a prison rule, I couldn't believe it. I couldn't forget Little Red.

Bob Fabian still had his column in the *Empire News.* I went to Barney Finnegan's in Fetter Lane and told Fabian all about Little Red. I asked him to write a piece about him in his column and told him about his brilliant naval record, how he had been torpedoed in the Atlantic and had shot his wife's lover when he returned home, how well behaved he was in jail. Fabian asked me for his full name and said he would think of an angle and give me a ring. Bob telephoned me the next day.

"You had me on, Ginger boy."

"What are you talking about, Bob?"

"The lifer you want me to write about." Bob even read me an old newspaper cutting. "The only navy your hero ever saw was at Cadet College, where he was a chef. His wife is still alive. He murdered two little girls who were gathering primroses in a wood."

Well, I didn't have much to say to that. "I'm sorry, Bob. He told me he had killed his old woman and I believed him." I decided not to bother about old lags any more, but I couldn't forget him.

About eighteen months afterwards I was driving along Kings Road, Chelsea, when I saw a little man going into a side turning. I felt sure it was Little Red Riding Hood. I drove round the next turning, doubled back on my tracks and pulled up just in front of him.

"Little Red," I called. He stopped and went white. I got out of the car and walked towards him. He went to shake hands, then looked nervous and stepped back. "Don't worry," I said.

He never said hello. His first words were, "The Prison Commissioners have been very good to me. I promised I wouldn't mix with criminals when they let me out last month. I'm in a hurry. I've got to get to work. I'm a prop man in the theatre." We arranged to meet the next day. Before he went I gave him a fiver. I called him back and explained it was not a Scottish one-pound note. He opened his little purse and pushed it in like a granny would. I asked him where he lived.

"Just down there with relations." Little Red took another right turn and disappeared.

He never turned up the next day. I had some beautiful clothes in the car which a little man called Bertie Wilkins, whom I had told about Little Red, had given me. It was Sunday evening. I was puzzled why he never turned up, and went to look for him. I wanted to take him out and give him a nice few quid. I looked in every pub in the Kings Road, but there was no Little Red. I went down the turning where I had seen him walking and took the first right he had taken. There were no houses, no flats, just one big, dimly-lit, ugly building. I never dreamed it existed in Chelsea. The doors were small like prison gates. I looked at the fancy name of what, when I was a kid, we used to call the workhouse. Little Red, after seventeen years and eight months in jail, was living in poverty in the workhouse. This is what he meant by the Commissioners being good to him. I rang the bell. An old man answered. He acted just like a prison gatekeeper.

"Have you got a man called Robinson here?" I knew that was the name Little Red was using.

He looked it up in the book. "No."

"Are you sure?"

Sure he was sure. He had been on the gate for twenty years. He looked a right goat, but was only another inmate. While I was arguing with this old goat a smartly dressed, nicely spoken young man came up and asked if he could help me. I called him on one side out of the ear of the old goat and told him who I was looking for and where he had come from. He knew Little Red, who had been passed into his care by the Prison Commissioners. He worked in the workhouse and got six shillings a week pocket money. He was allowed out till ten p.m.

"He's around somewhere in Chelsea. He's quiet and never speaks to anyone."

I drove out of Sydney Street and decided I would look in one more pub. I pushed open the door of the public bar, which was empty. Sitting just behind the door was Little Red with a pint in his hand which was empty and gazing into an empty fireplace just as I used to see him at Dartmoor with wandering eyes and a pint of cocoa. I went straight to the counter.

"Come and have a drink." Reluctantly he agreed. I never told him I knew his secret.

"I am an ex-lifer on licence and can be recalled. The Prison Commissioners have been very good to me. They said I mustn't mix with criminals."

It was hard to make him smile. I offered him some more money. He declined. I realised I was upsetting him, and gave him my phone number.

"If I can help you, just ring." As a parting shot I asked him, "Tell me, did you ever find another Mother Bear?"

He smiled for the first time.

"The best Mother Bear I had in seventeen years was Jim the Penman."

I left the pub with a lump in my throat. Little Red was suffering from jail rot. He did not stay long in Chelsea Workhouse. He couldn't get a ticket for the membership he needed to work in the world he loved, the theatre, the world of Mother Bear. For a time he wandered round the country. Then one day he did what Pierrepoint had failed to do for him. He hanged himself in a bedsitter in South London.

A lot of old lags commit suicide.

Joseph Kinsella, the first man I met when I was received into Dartmoor to begin my life sentence, also hanged himself after leaving jail, where he had served ten years for blackmail.

His co-defendant accomplice was a man called Harry Raymond, who had been an actor. He was a good-looking fellow and well spoken. Just before Christmas I nipped into a store in Oxford Street to buy two kids a present. I saw Father Christmas and his lucky dip and after buying them their presents I went to get a couple of extra ones from his barrel. I looked up.

"What's your game, Father Christmas?" It was Harry Raymond, who had just come out from doing ten.

"Don't talk to me," he said. "Don't talk to me. You'll get

me the sack. I got myself a job for Christmas. Keeps me out of trouble."

"Don't worry about getting the sack. Hang on here."

"The manager's walking up towards me now. Don't talk to me."

When I saw Harry patting little boys' bottoms and telling them to put their hand in the old lucky dip I wondered to myself. I don't think he ever went in for little boys, but he was as queer as a coot. Anyway, it was a good story for me. I had found the best Father Christmas in Oxford Street that Christmas.

I telephoned for a photographer.

"Harry, you don't want to worry about getting the sack," I said when I went back into the store. "Your wages are going to be two hundred and fifty pounds this weekend."

We started taking pictures of him dressed up in his Father Christmas uniform fast and furiously. I am happy to say that Harry had a good Christmas and in the New Year I sold his series. Being a gambler, Harry went away and turned it into quite a lot of money. He got himself a new boyfriend and a nice apartment. Then he went broke again. He either had to work or revert back to crime, his being blackmail, and that could eventually mean jail. Harry didn't relish returning to jail. They found him dead, sitting on a chair in Hyde Park. He'd taken an overdose.

Harry always used to enjoy reading my plays and he gave me encouragement.

"When you get out of here, son, you've got no need to worry. You'll always get a living. You've got talent, boy. I wish I had it."

"Time will tell, time will tell," I used to say.

13

"Sign here, sir"

I decided that I had had enough of journalism. I wanted to be a writer. I wanted to write scripts. It was a hard world to break into. With the money I had saved up through journalism I decided to go into business. When I had enough money I could just turn it up and go back to writing, writing the things that I wanted to write, the way I wanted to write them, and I could visit the countries I wanted to see.

I fancied the car business and managed to get hold of a very small site facing the Old Vic, a corner site just big enough for an advertising board with a little bit of wire round it. It was part of a large site. I took a chance, had a fencing firm fence in the lot all the way round and squatted. I opened up an office on the site. I knew nothing about the car game, but went to two friends of mine. They took one look at the site.

"Main road, this is it, Jimmy. Any help we can give you we'll give you." They advised me that the best thing I could do was to try and get permission for petrol, which would make the site very valuable. I called it Waterloo Autos.

I used to go and buy my motor-cars from Warren Street in Euston and, despite my criminal convictions, well respected dealers never hesitated to give me a few thousand pounds' credit.

On Saturday afternoon my squatting caught up with me. A nice Jewish gentleman called on the site and asked:

"What are you doing on my land?"

"Your land, sir? I've got a lease on this from a company."

"A company? This belongs to me."

"What, all of it, sir?"

"Well, all of it except that piece in the corner."

"Well, I've been conned. My poor old Mum . . . Scrubbing floors . . . What am I going to do?"

"How much profit do you get on those cars?" he asked.

"Oooooh . . . about a fiver."

"Well, not to worry, laddie, not to worry. I'll get in touch. I just happened to be driving by. I haven't been past here for years. I used to have a kosher butcher's shop along here in a row of shops, but it was bombed during the war."

"Oh, yes, sir," I said.

Years ago crooked people used to describe themselves as bookmaker's clerks when they were arrested by the police. As the years went by they described themselves as motor-car dealers and lately as company directors. Sometimes there were more people described as car dealers but who knew nothing whatsoever about the business than there were car dealers. That is how the business got a bad name. They have a saying in Warren Street, "Let your eyes be your guide and the money be the last thing you part with." Warren Street dealers rarely sold their cars to the public. They sold to other dealers whose eyes were their guide.

Some of the happiest days of my life were spent in Warren Street. I had lot of fun and lots of laughs and met some great guys. But they were sufferers. I should think that every old lag who came out from doing a long sentence came to Warren Street. They knew that these people were simpatico and would never let an old lag go away without a few quid. They never refused, they would never say no.

I started to learn about property dealers and hire-purchase. I began to get a social conscience when I saw how the public were being exploited by hire-purchase companies. The railway employee was borrowing money from the finance company. The finance company was borrowing money from the railway employee's pension fund. It was going round in a vicious circle. In the whole of my three or four years as a car dealer I never saw a single working man read the hire-purchase forms. I couldn't even read them myself, the print was so small.

"Sign here, sir." They would sign. I used to get them to initial each page and each paragraph.

The finance companies were unscrupulous. They just fixed their own rates of interest as it suited them, eleven and a half, twelve per cent. If a man defaulted on a couple of payments they gave him no mercy, even if he was unemployed. They saw plenty of profit in a cheap car if a man had made quite a number of payments, and used to employ snatch-back men to snatch the cars back.

Old lags used to visit me all the time. They just drove me mad, but I couldn't say no. They knew where to find me. A character came in one day and asked if Jimmy O'Connor was here.

"No, he's not here at the moment. Can I help you? I work for him," I said.

"Oh, he's a great pal of mine," he said. "I was in the next cell to him for ten years."

"Well, what do you want?"

"I thought he might be able to help me. I need a bit of expenses to get down to Bognor. If I can get down there someone's going to give me a car which is worth three or four hundred quid. I thought maybe he'd buy it off me and give me the money to go down and collect it."

"Yeah, well, if you come back this afternoon you may see him here." I knew I wouldn't be there.

That afternoon I left for the South of France with a man called Sam Norman, a self-made cockney millionaire who used to manufacture juke boxes called Bel Ami. He had one factory in Ilford and another in France. He had a twin-engined Heron plane and a pilot, but he could fly it himself.

Sam always had a suite at the Carlton and his yacht, the *Bel Ami*, would be tied up in the harbour. He used to stand on the balcony above the porch of the Carlton and shout to me on the beach in his cockney vernacular, "Jim, get the Chris craft out."

I used to go along the beach with a camera taking pictures of some of the darlings, and then I would invite them aboard *my* yacht. Sam's captain was a good guy. Away we used to go to little islands to sunbathe or sometimes we would sail down to Portofino. It was another side of life for me, a new experience.

Some old pals were down there, too. I looked round the beach one day and counted about a hundred years from Dartmoor. Another night, sitting on the terrace outside the Carlton, I heard two cat burglars having an argument, over their large gin fizzes, as to who was the best cat burglar. I couldn't believe it. While I was down there they had a few good tickles and robbed some villas for a nice few thousand. They went further than that. After disposing of their jewellery, they went down to the Casino and won some more. They picked up a couple of birds and at about five o'clock in the morning went to bed in their hotel. At about lunchtime they woke up. One of them stretched across for his lighter. The birds were still in bed. He jumped out, put the lights on and found his trousers were gone. They looked round. Everything had gone, all their money, all their clothes. They had been robbed. They did hoot. They couldn't believe it had happened to them. Two of the best burglars in London had been robbed.

They had to ring down to tell the hotel manager and he had no alternative but to call in the police, who took them to some caves at the back of Cannes. Spread out on the rocks drying were their brand-new clothes, some of them not even worn. A couple of Algerians were arrested. They tried to talk to them with their eyes. They told me, "It was diabolical the way the coppers knocked them about. They belted the life out of them."

Back in London, in the grey mist of Waterloo Road, I was still hoping to get my petrol permit. Other people had already tried unsuccessfully six times, and I was appealing against the London County Council decision on a site on which I was actually still only a squatter. Waiting for the appeal decision was getting me down. I used to sit in the office thinking about the world I wanted to get back into, writing. I still dabbled a bit in journalism and series. I went to the office one morning. It was always misty and murky in the morning and there was the usual stream of traffic and mass of grey faces passing my office window.

An old lag worked for me because I like old lags. Joe used to pray for rain because I used to call him into the office out of the wet. He'd had enough rain in Dartmoor. We used to sit gazing out of the window and have a nobble and a laugh while hoping that somebody would come and buy a motor-car. For sure, anyone who walks round a site in the pissing rain is a certain punter for a car.

On this particular morning I saw a little gentleman looking at a big American car. 'A nut case,' I thought to myself. Who wants a drop-head coupé in the pissing rain? Nevertheless, the prospect of taking one hundred pounds profit out of the big old beast was too much for me. It did about eight to the gallon.

"Shift yourself, Joe. There's a mug outside at the Yank."

I watched Joe through the rain-spattered window waving his arms about. I thought he must be guaranteeing the motor for the rest of its natural life. He was an ex-con man, now going straight, and the best salesman in the motor business. Then I saw him shrug his shoulders and the little gentleman departed wetter but wiser. My heart sank when I thought of the one that got away, one hundred pounds in cold blood. Joe returned to the office.

"Well, you must be slipping."

"No," answered Joe. "It's an old lag just come out from doing ten years this morning, or so he said. He wanted to put the bite on you for a few quid, I suppose. I told him you weren't here, guv'nor. He told me to tell you, just to say that Midgie called."

"Midgie? My God!"

I sent Joe running out into the rain to look for him. I hadn't recognised Midgie through the streaming window. I'd never seen him in civilian clothes before, only in prison grey. I had worked with him in Dartmoor and Parkhurst and couldn't he make a trumpet speak! He was number one trumpet player in the prison band. Midgie had never had much time for civilian clothes. He was sixty-odd years old and had spent thirty-five years in jail. It was home to him.

Midgie learnt the rudiments of music at an industrial school. By the time he got to Borstal he could play the scales. After his sixth lagging he could play like Louis Armstrong but always on a borrowed trumpet. He changed his religion to Salvationist so that he could cadge one, but no luck. He tried them all, but to no avail. It was "Nearer my trumpet to me" than "Nearer my God". He was the only man I knew who had seven religions and no God. He used to say he would become a Jew to get a trumpet, but I knew that in his heart of hearts he was an atheist. I met him doing his seventh lagging. He always used to tell me that he'd give himself the best trumpet in the world some day.

I was glad that Joe found him. We shook hands. I sent Joe down the road to have a drink. He did like a tot. I apologised to Midgie for not recognising him under his civilian trilby. When old lags came to me I used to give them a pound for every year in jail they had done. I slipped him a tenner, thinking I would put it on the price of the next car I settled. Midgie was indignant.

"No. I want a job so I can save up for a trumpet and go busking with the one-legged mob in Oxford Street."

I explained to him that I couldn't employ another old lag, but I said, "I'll see what can be done." I found him a place to sleep and he left clutching a tenner and full of good cheer.

"Come back any time. I'm here," I said.

Joe came back from the boozer.

"What does he want? A job or a bob?"

I laughed. "No, he's an old fellow sufferer. I've known him for years. In actual fact, when he was doing his last five I wrote a letter for him to the colliery manager of Durham. It went something like this:

> Dear Sir,
>
> I shall be finishing a sentence of five years next month and I was wondering if you could see your way clear to giving me a job at the mine. I have been number one trumpet player in the prison band on my last five sentences. I also played in the Newcastle Colliery Band once for three months.

The manager wrote back:

> Dear Sir,
>
> We appreciate your difficulties. Re your recent application for employment on leaving prison from which we gather you are a good trumpet player, we would be very happy to give this further consideration if you can tell us what work you can do.

That afternoon Jimmy Marney called in at my site. He often used to pop in. Jim was a good bookmaker, not a crooked man, who used to live near the Waterloo Road. He understood the ways of the homeless wrongdoer. He used to see them day and night marching into the Salvation Army Hostel at the Elephant and Castle. I told him about old Midge and it turned out he had a friend who ran a one-man mail-order business in children's toys. He wanted someone to help him parcel them up and arranged that Midge should get a job, with a bed in the office into the bargain.

A week went by and Jim Marney came to see me, shaking his head.

"Nice, isn't it? Thanks very much."

"What's the matter?"

"I've been away racing for a few days. What do you think's happened?"

"I don't know. Tell me."

"Your little pal. He's nicked all the postage money and the float."

"How much?"

"Forty-eight quid."

"Did he take anything else?"

"No, but my friend's got a dead needle and has called the coppers in," said Jim.

"What? Midge's wanted." I felt sick. There was no need to call the police in for forty-eight blinking quid. I would gladly have repaid it myself, but it was too late now.

Some days later Midgie wrote to me from Brixton Prison. I got to the sessions on the day he was weighed off. He didn't mess about. He broke the eleventh commandment again and went straight in and pleaded guilty. He didn't want anybody to defend him. He didn't seem to mind. The Clerk of the Court asked him if he had anything to say.

"No," he answered.

So they called the probation officer who had known him for six years. He said that on release from prison six weeks before, arrangements had been made for him to go into an old people's home, but he hadn't arrived and they had had no news of him until he was arrested.

"He says he doesn't like the idea of going into a home," said the probation officer. "He left prison with thirty shillings in his pocket and seems to have wandered aimlessly since. The police tell me that when he was arrested he had in his possession fourpence. He tells me that he would like to go back to prison for the rest of his life as he cannot adjust himself to being free. He has twenty-four previous convictions."

"Well, well," said the Chairman. "This seems to be one of those rare cases where we have no alternative. You must go to prison for twelve years."

I was choked. At four o'clock when the court rose I went down to the cells to see him. I could hardly speak, but Midgie was smiling.

"I hope that old Ambrosini is still bandmaster at the Moor," then changing quickly to back slang, he slipped me a brief. The brief was a ticket for the Waterloo left-luggage office.

"Do me a favour, Jim. Send it on to me at the Moor."

We said our goodbyes and I left a far sadder man than he was. I sent Joe down to Waterloo station to collect the parcel. About an hour afterwards he came back a bit pissed. We opened it up. There it was, shining like the Koh-i-noor diamond, a brand-new sparkling trumpet together with a receipt, the sum—forty-eight pounds. Today Midgie is the happiest trumpeter in the land or in Her Majesty's prisons. Of course, I sent the bloody thing on to him at Dartmoor. Well, wouldn't you?

14

Her name was Nemone Lethbridge

Back at the office I discovered a notice informing me that my appeal was going to be heard the following week. That night I closed the place up, drove over Westminster Bridge into Belgrave Square to the Star Tavern. While I was there, Sir Lionel Thomson, a barrister, came in with a very attractive young lady, also a member of the Bar. She had come from her chambers and wasn't the type of person who used pubs, but she wanted to see a programme of Brian Horrocks who was a great friend of her father's. I found myself sitting between the television and this attractive young lady.

"Would you like me to move, Miss? Would you like to come where I am?"

"It's quite all right," she said. "It's quite all right."

"No, just come and sit up here and no one can't get in your way."

"I just want to watch this. It finishes in another thirty minutes."

"Of course. No one over here will interfere with you."

When the programme finished I started to talk to her. Her name was Nemone Lethbridge. Sir Lionel came across.

"Nemone, this is the character I was telling you about, Jimmy O'Connor. He's a very interesting man. You should talk to him."

He didn't want to worry about that. I'd already been talking to her. We discussed crime and juvenile delinquency. She told me she was writing a book about Doggie, Lord Goddard, ghosting it for his Clerk. I said I would like to read the proof when she had finished it. She left. I said good night.

A few weeks went by and one Sunday I found a letter from Nemone Lethbridge telling me that she had finished her book and was having a party the following Wednesday. If I could find the time I was most welcome. Would I telephone if I wasn't coming as she would like to read the script that I had told her about and partly written.

I telephoned the number and spoke to one of her friends, a girl who had been at Oxford with Nemone. She told me that she was out, that she had gone to Mass. I asked which church.

"St Mary of the Angels," she told me.

I wasn't waiting for the party on Wednesday. I looked at my watch, jumped into the car and drove like mad to the church. I stood at the back until I saw her coming down the aisle. Then I walked out of the church and met her outside. She looked beautiful. I asked her whether I could take her to lunch.

"Why go to lunch?" she said. "We're cooking lunch at home. Come and join us."

She shared a house with Xanthe Wakefield, Lord Wakefield's daughter, a brilliant woman who had a double first at Oxford and worked on the B.B.C. "Tonight" programme with Cliff Michelmore. I enjoyed that Sunday lunch. It was a pleasure to talk to all of them because they were out of my world.

I went to the party the following Wednesday. Lionel Thomson was there. I think he was a sort of minder at the time because maybe they were a bit nervous of me. There were many members of the Bar there as well as people from the literary and arts world and another beautiful barrister, Anne Curnow, Nemone's closest friend and now the first woman Treasury Counsel.

The party was breaking up and I was about to leave. They asked me to stay. Four or five of us stayed and we laughed and joked. I think I amused them with my cockney vernacular. One thing I didn't have was an inferiority complex with these people. I found that they had more in common with the working class than the so-called swells of the middle class. They had been sent away to boarding schools, public schools and then to university. I suppose being sent to public school is in some ways no different from being sent to Borstal. In fact, Nemone told me they used to have a dish at her school on Sunday nights called Borstal Pie.

I arranged to take her out to dinner the following week and during that week I had a bit of good news. I had been given my petrol permission. That piece of paper was worth twenty thousand pounds. It was now a matter of picking the right time and the right company to sell it to. News of granted petrol permissions travelled very, very fast. On the second day a little short dark gypsy-looking man pulled up in his car and walked in.

"Good morning. Nice place you've got here. Do you like my suit? I've just been down the tailor's down the Cut in Lambeth. Good tailor. I was passing here and thought I'd look at your site. Do you want to sell it?"

"Well—" I said, thinking about it. "My name's Jimmy O'Connor."

"I know it is."

"What's yours?" I asked.

"Oliver Cutts."

"Oh, I've heard about you," I said. "You've got all those petrol stations in South London."

He didn't mess about. He took one look at the site and he made me a good offer. After a little bit of arguing I got a bit more. I made a phone call to a man (Jack Fishman) who had said he would lend me the money to buy the site, on which I was still squatting, once I had the petrol permission. I sold the place to Oliver Cutts and gave half the money to Jack Fishman.

I carried on in the car business for a time, but Nemone had read my play. She told me I should open it up and turn it into a musical, that I shouldn't be in the car business, that I could write, that I was a very good writer and I should stick to writing. I told her this had been my ambition for years.

I introduced her to a new world and she started taking me out to dinner parties. The first time I didn't know how to eat, and had to watch the other people to see what tool they were picking up. I wondered why they had given me a gin and tonic with the asparagus.

"Take that back, mate."

"That's the finger-bowl, sir."

I didn't care really.

I took a flat in Kensington Court, by Hyde Park. Nemone often used to come and cook for me, but she was dedicated to her profession and always went to bed early. At about half past nine at night, home she would go. I must confess I used to go out because I liked to drink.

By this time I had fallen in love with Nemone, but I thought marriage was out of the question. You can't mix chalk with cheese. Nemone is a very family-minded person and was brought up that way.

Her grandfather, Sir John Maynard, was the Vice-Chancellor of Quetta University in India. Her grandmother was an American from the Appomatox where the peace treaty was signed at the end of the Civil War. Her father was a professional soldier. He was Slim's right-hand man in Burma during Operation SOB ("Shit or Bust", he told me). He was the Chief of Intelligence during the Occupation in Berlin. As a child Nemone used to go into Hitler's bunker and visit Spandau jail.

At Camberley they named a college Lethbridge College after her father.

When I met Nemone he was head of the Civil Defence for the West Country and all the Chief Constables of the West Country used to visit her home.

A man like that would naturally be alarmed if his daughter were to marry a barrow boy and convicted murderer. Who can blame him? I wouldn't like myself as a son-in-law.

I proposed marriage to Nemone. She explained some of the family difficulties and refused. She had already checked with the Chief Constable of Bath, an ex-London C.I.D. man, to find out whether I was really a straight person. He must have made a good report on me. I had a history of work since my release from jail and worked seven days a week, every day of the year. Christmas meant nothing to me. I had spent eleven of them in prisons. Christmas still means nothing to me. It is for children. Father Christmas climbs down the chimney on Christmas Eve and brings them presents. He climbs down for grown-ups too, but he climbs straight up again on Boxing Day. The hail fellow well met, the cigars, and the arms round the shoulders, and then your fellow men are stabbing you in the back and twisting the knives. Christmas and good cheer is all over.

One evening in July 1959 I had just bought a car in Chelsea, and called into the Marlborough, Ben Slennett's pub at the back of Sloane Street Police Station. As I walked in, the missus of the pub said, "They've got him, then."

"Got who?"

"The man who shot the policeman."

"Oh, yes," I said. "Where is he?"

"He's across the road."

The Marlborough was a policemen's pub. Quite a lot of policemen from Chelsea Police Station used it. I often used to drink there with Bruce Reynolds and a couple of the other Great

Train Robbers. They were younger and used to look up to me because I had served a long time. Bruce Reynolds was bright, intelligent and well read. We used to discuss literature, politics, and, of course, the police. We sat in the corner and used to see them come in. Some of the old-time coppers knew me and used to give me a nod. Ben Slennett would break his ankle to talk to a policeman. He just couldn't help it.

On the Monday of this particular week Guenther Podola, a professional German criminal, shot Sergeant Purdy. I knew Purdy, a nice guy. There was no doubt about Podola's guilt. He shot Purdy in cold blood. When they arrested him on Thursday, July 16th, they did not know whether a man was sitting behind the door with a loaded gun; whether they heard a click or not doesn't matter, and it's still debated as to what took place in that room. It's quite simple. Podola got a belting. But that should have been the end of it. They should have taken him off to the station and charged him to be held until his trial to take the punishment due to him.

I was standing at the bar and in came a copper I knew. He was complaining that young uniformed P.C.s were coming in on duty, going into the cell and still belting Guenther Podola.

"Why don't you stop it, then?"

"We will have to."

I was annoyed when I heard about the continued beating. So were a couple of C.I.D. men because it would be down to them. Two or three more came in, also upset. They had to have large ones. On some occasions it must be a bastard job being a policeman, finding the mutilated bodies of women and children with their heads battered in or objects stuffed into their innards. You can't really love your fellow men. That's why policemen are sometimes different from the ordinary person.

I had to meet Nemone just past her chambers at the Aldwych. I picked her up as inconspicuously as possible, walking along with her blue bag over her shoulder carrying her wig and gown and her law books.

As we drove across London to her home in Bayswater she saw on the placards that the police had arrested a man for the shooting of a policeman. I told her I had just come from the Marlborough Arms and told her about Podola's belting. We decided on a campaign that evening. I suggested that someone should instruct a lawyer to go straight to the station on Podola's behalf and represent this foreigner who had only arrived in England a few days previously, to see at least that he got a fair crack of the whip.

My journalist's mind thought that tomorrow morning Podola might be dead, and I guessed that that night he would be transferred to a hospital. I telephoned a newspaper that same night and one of their staff reporters went to see the Home Secretary, Rab Butler. That evening Podola was transferred to St Stephen's Hospital where he stayed for a few days under constant police observation. At the end of that time, Dr Harvey, the Consultant Physician, told the police that Podola was not fit to be interviewed.

In Nemone's chambers was a woman barrister called Margaret Puxsom whose husband, Maurice Williams, was a solicitor. Etiquette said that he had to be retained by someone. We contacted someone on the *Daily Sketch* and they put up a front man to retain Maurice Williams. I suggested that Fred Lawton, now a High Court judge, should defend Podola because he was a good fighter at the time.

The doctor who examined Podola just after four o'clock on the sixteenth of July found it impossible to make any contact with him. He couldn't get through to Podola. He couldn't get Podola to say anything. Podola could only just open his mouth. The doctor thought he was recovering from a possible concussion and was withdrawn from reality. He appeared dazed and exhausted. Either he could not, or he was being cunning and would not talk.

I told Maurice Williams that I had to set the ball rolling and made the facts known to the people who ought to know. I suggested that Podola's defence might be retrograde amnesia, a genuine loss of memory which would in effect mean that he was unfit to plead while he was still suffering from amnesia.

Maurice Williams got himself emotionally involved with this case. It was his first big chance, a murder case. The story was put out that he was retained by a group of anonymous business men a couple of days earlier to defend Podola. This was a lot of old nonsense. A newspaper paid for the preliminary defence at least.

Then Maurice Williams told me that Podola was playing chess in hospital. I thought his case for amnesia was gone for a burton. If you can't remember the past you can't remember how to do certain things. You can remember how to clean your teeth or your shoes, but with genuine amnesia you wouldn't remember how to play chess or pontoon with the policemen who were looking after you. I have lived with lunatics and murderers for many years of my life. I have been with a man who had amnesia and had more opportunity to study him than any prison doctor.

I was always on the side of the person, no matter who they had killed, if I thought they were going to be hanged. If they were going to receive a heavy sentence, then I minded my own business. I wasn't doing anything for Podola. As far as I was concerned, I was just doing it to save another person from being hanged. The abolition of the death penalty has worked things out much better, as the police themselves will one day realise. Members of a jury were often reluctant to return a verdict of guilty, even for the shooting of a policeman, when they knew that the accused could be hanged.

That night Nemone and I decided to get married. Our plans had to be kept secret because Nemone knew she would be ostracised by her profession if they knew she was marrying an old lag. I told only a few close friends. One day I was at a wedding party with two pals, Teddy and Charlie. They were writing cheques as gifts.

"Might as well write me one," I said.

"Why?" said Teddy. "Who's going to marry 'The Lifer'?"

"With a face as ugly as yours," Charlie added.

I think I blushed. "That little girl you met the other night. . . ."

It took them a while to swallow that, then Charlie said, "But why all the secrecy?"

I told them it was because Nemone was a barrister and I wasn't the greatest gift in the world.

"Cor blimey," they both said. "You're telling us."

I also told Jack Fishman, who had been a friend since I left jail. I asked him to be my best man. One of Nemone's friends, a barrister, was the bridesmaid.

Off we flew to Dublin on the eve of the Feast of the Assumption. The best man was no problem. He was teetotal, but after we'd almost cleaned the Gresham out of champagne the rest of the stag party moved on. We gravitated towards the tough end of Dublin, and in a bar jammed with Friday night Irishmen somebody spilled Teddy's drink.

"He'll apologise," said Teddy.

"He'll murder you," said Charlie.

"Look," I said. "There's two hundred Irishmen here. They'll murder the lot of us."

"He'll apologise," said Teddy.

"Teddy, please," I said. "I've come here to get married, not to finish up in Mountjoy Prison."

Next morning we waited at the Cathedral, and we waited and we waited. Timing was never the Irishman's best point, and somebody at the Cathedral had, as Teddy said, "got too many runners on the card".

Hundreds of Italians were milling around waiting for a special Mass which was nearly an hour late already so that our wedding would be later.

Nemmie drove round and round the Cathedral with Teddy and Charlie and her bridesmaid in a taxi, while Jack Fishman and I kept nipping in and out of the Cathedral. Then the cab stopped and Charlie got out to tell us, "If you don't stop Teddy arguing with this cabby about the Six Counties there'll be a blooming riot."

"That's all we're short of," I said, looking at my watch again.

Charlie joined us, and then Teddy noticed that everybody who walked past the Cathedral made the sign of the cross.

"Bet you the next three guys that come by do that," he said.

"Make it a pony (£25)," said Charlie.

The next two were priests, so that was all right. Then came a man smoking a cigarette and reading the racing edition. He was just about to cross himself when he dropped his cigarette, bent to pick it up and walked on without doing it. So Teddy lost his pony.

The cab came round once again. We were very late now, and I said, "You know what? We're not going to get married today after all." Arrangements had gone cockeyed. Our priest was busy in another chapel and still had a Mass for hundreds of Italians before he got to us. When she should have been saying 'I do', Nemmie was still driving round and round Dublin's Pro-Cathedral. I waited outside for an hour, then I darted in and out for another twenty minutes, panicking in case Nemone got fed up with the whole thing and called it off.

Then the organ pealed and Nemone came down the aisle. She

was wearing green, not because of her Irish ancestry or mine, but because she liked it.

The mixed up arrangements were lucky, because instead of a plain and simple wedding, without asking us a choir of thirty Italians sang the Nuptial Mass. Their voices were glorious. If I'd never understood before why people weep at weddings I did then.

The only discord came from my old cockney chum, Teddy. Not being a Catholic, he didn't understand Holy Communion and kept mumbling, "What's this, then?" and "Here, what're you eating all them little sweets for?"

Most of the hotel had finished lunch when we started the wedding breakfast. Page boys kept invading us, "Paging Father O'Connor", but we saw through Teddy and Charlie's game when they paged "Father O'Fishman".

Finally we left for our honeymoon on the coast of Connemara and on a little island called Innisboffin off the west coast of Ireland. Our honeymoon was nearly over when we saw a friend of Nemone's on a beach. We started across to him, then changed our minds and walked the other way in case he asked any questions.

Finally, I gave up the car business. The B.B.C. were going to start a new series called "The Wednesday Play". James MacTaggart, the producer, read *Three Clear Sundays*, liked it and accepted it. I was very happy and went on the piss, but at the Star Tavern in Belgrave Mews I had another shock.

Kevin McLory, the producer of *Thunderball*, had just flown in from New York. He congratulated me on the good news.

"What good news?"

"I read in the *New York Times* that you were married to Nemone Lethbridge."

We had been able to keep it a secret for three years to protect Nemone's career. Even when journalists checked the records at Somerset House they could find no evidence that we were married. But, finally, a well-informed reporter with contacts in Dublin discovered that that was where we were married. Some of the Sundays were about to do a story, so I went to Cecil King's office on Saturday morning to deliver a letter. Friends of mine also approached the Rothermere group and were able to suppress the story from that angle. Cecil King telephoned me at home. In the letter I had told him that we all had skeletons in the cupboard. The editors still wonder today how I managed to kill that story.

Unfortunately, it finally broke in New York and I had no chance of suppressing the story six thousand miles away.

The head of Nemone's chambers felt that because she was married to a criminal it would discredit her colleagues and the whole of the chambers. He wrote her a fourteen-page letter suggesting she resign and advising her to go away for a holiday to think about it.

With Nemone and her mother I travelled round Greece. When we returned to Athens there was a letter waiting at the King George Hotel for Nemone from Ian Percival, head of her chambers, in which he told her that he had removed her name from the door of the chambers.

She broke down and cried. She loved the profession and felt that she had been ostracised and forced out because of her marriage. It was then that I regretted marrying her. I felt that I had destroyed something beautiful—but physically and mentally I could not resist her.

15

"*You're all* my material"

She was a brilliant barrister. On five occasions she defended the Kray twins. On five occasions they were found not guilty. She defended Frank Mitchell, who was eventually murdered himself, for attempted murder.

One evening we went to see Joan Littlewood's *Oh What a Lovely War* at Stratford.

I asked Nemone, "Do you want to eat before we go or afterwards?"

"I don't mind. I'll leave it to you."

I thought she's got a shock coming to her now. I had just passed a pie-and-mash shop. Eels and mash are my favourite. I couldn't resist it.

"Would you mind if I take you in here?"

There were marble-topped tables with bowls of eels lying about and big salt and pepper pots. Nemone had never seen this before and didn't like the look of the eels. I had a couple of bowls and mash and Nemone messed about with a pie, but she laughed and enjoyed it.

At the theatre, sitting in the front row, were Ronnie and Reggie Kray and half a dozen of the chaps with their blue mohair suits, high-necked white shirts and their little white handkerchiefs sticking out of their top pockets. We were just behind them.

"Nemone, they won't sit through this show," I said.

After the interval, as I forecast, the twins and the firm didn't return. When the curtain went down we went behind to have a drink with George Sewell Jnr and some of the cast. Drinks were sent across from the bar at the club from Reggie, Ronnie and the firm. Most of them were youngsters. They all nodded. I stood with my back against the wall and just smiled at them.

Ronnie came across.

"Hello, Ginge, how are you?"

I don't think he knew that Nemone was my wife, but he made an announcement.

"Miss Lethbridge, on behalf of one and all of the family, we wish to raise a toast to you for all you've done for us and for getting us acquitted." And in unison they said, "Cheers, Miss Lethbridge."

Cheers, I thought, isn't it nice! Then they invited Nemone and myself to a benefit for some charitable organisation. They put it about that Lord Snowdon and Princess Margaret were coming and they had the red carpet laid down at their club, the Double R.

I advised Nemone not to get involved socially with the Krays. They used to try and make social contacts and then exploit them, making sure they always had press coverage, even if it was only a local paper. In fact, they used to employ a P.R.O.

One day the twins invited Nemone with the Managing Clerk of the firm of solicitors back to have a cup of coffee and to meet Ma and Pa at Roman Row. Without ever having been there, I described the house to Nemone.

"Was there red-and-gold wallpaper? Was there a bar that lit up?"

"Yes," she said. "Yes."

Two or three of the firm were there and apparently there was a conference in each room. They gave her a bunch of flowers and an envelope. Inside was five hundred pounds. She gave it back to them.

"I can't take that."

They didn't understand. They left and one came back.

"I'm very sorry, Miss Lethbridge, in front of all those people," He tried to give it to her again.

"No, I'll take the flowers, thank you," she said, and got the Managing Clerk to take her away from Roman Row.

With some Gilbert and Sullivan operas and Maundy Gregory in mind, I have watched the new affluent society milk pension funds to make fortunes out of hire-purchase companies. I have watched the bourgeoisie living in neo-Georgian-type houses with their Rolls-Royces and their wives in mink coats going to night-clubs on a Friday night, something new in their lives, or in their wives' lives anyway. I have seen the snobbery there is among certain self-made men, how they want to rub shoulders with the so-called upper classes with toppers and tails and boxes at Ascot and marquees on the lawn and after-Ascot champers parties.

On one occasion there was a right punch up at the after-Ascot party. One fellow in his topper and tails met a character called The Badger.

"Listen you, what about that money you owe me? Five hundred quid."

"What are you talking about?"

The host came up. "Leave off, for God's sake leave off. I've got directors of finance companies here."

"Never mind about that." All of a sudden there was a battle royal. Toppers and tails went flying. The tent was going in and out. Over went the table and the champagne glasses, and the host, trying to sound like a swell, said, "Would you mind getting off my property and leaving this place at once? You should be ashamed of yourself. You weren't invited to this place anyway." They'd only pushed a barrow together for most of their lives, the two of them!

This is how I came to write *Tap on the Shoulder* about a character I created from many people I had observed. I poured them all into the Irish stewpot and produced *Tap on the Shoulder*. The Queen taps you on the shoulder when she knights you and Old Bill from the Yard taps you on the shoulder when he nicks you.

I was very lucky with the team around me at the B.B.C. Roger Smith and Tony Garnett were both ordinary working-class boys who had been to university. Jimmy MacTaggart was the producer and Ken Loach gave as much to directing my plays as I gave to writing the script. I took him around and introduced him to the real McCoy. He met his characters in real life.

Four or five film companies tried to sign me up for the film rights of my next three plays. The first even went as far as registering one of my plays without even discussing it with me or signing a contract. I took one look at his Rolls-Royce, took the number and checked with Hire Purchase Information for which I had a code name, 'Cobblers'. There was a few grand owing on the H.P. I thought I'm not leaving this little team at the B.B.C. for the type of film producer who drives around in Rolls-Royces on hire-purchase. I preferred a director with holes in his sleeves and Sellotape round his glasses to the tycoons of Wardour Street.

One night in October 1965 I went with one of the unconvicted train robbers to The Pheasantry in the Kings Road. I had no transport and at about half past one in the morning a young man invited me to a party in Notting Hill Gate. I accepted because at least I was near home.

"It's just a cockney party, Ginger."

"That's all right. I haven't been to one for years."

I didn't want to lose touch. I enjoyed that party, but I had a bit of a shock that night. A man called Ernest Thomas was there. He greeted me and after a couple of drinks he told me that he knew I was innocent, that he knew who the murderer was and that one day he would tell me the man's name. As soon as he mentioned my case I realised that he had been a very close friend of Mr A, the man Flo Sayers had lived with at the time of the murder and who had been living opposite me in Paddington years later, soon after my release. I took him into the garden and pleaded with him to tell me how he knew who the murderer was. He told me that Mr A had given him a few quid the morning after the murder and had confessed to the murder. Later they went to see some friends and Ernest Thomas said he was glad he lost the money playing dice.

In November 1965, Ernest Thomas made a statement to my solicitor, David Napley. "Mr A is the man who did it. He came round to me the next morning and told me he did it. I said, 'Why tell me a thing like that? I don't want to know a thing like that.' He said, 'I had to tell somebody. It is on my conscience.'

"I remember thinking it was a bit of a liberty that Jimmy was in there, but once he got reprieved we said forget it. If it had come to hanging it would have been different."

At Christmas a year later I went to San Francisco to visit my son, his wife and two children, and on the way back I met George Sewell's son, Danny, in New York. We went to P. J. Clarke's Bar.

Back in London, I telephoned George Sewell and gave him messages from his son in New York. I invited him to my home and arranged that he should come on Friday, 6th, at about lunchtime. I also contacted a detective agency. They installed wiring in my flat and joined it up to my study at the other side of the building. The detectives arrived at ten forty-five a.m. and locked themselves in the study. Much to my disappointment, George Sewell Senior arrived with his son George. I wanted him on his own. I tried to talk about my case. George Sewell Senior said he did not want to discuss it. His son pointed to Nemone and said to his father:

"But maybe she does."

Then he confessed to committing perjury. When he had gone I discussed the recording with the private detectives.

Sewell came into a pub in Fleet Street one day where I was having a drink with Peter Earl, a top crime reporter I've known for many years. He admitted in the presence of Peter that he had been forced to commit perjury by the police because they had threatened him.

In the meantime, 1967 was a lucky year for me. Ken Loach was given the award for best director of the year for a play of mine called *The Coming Out Party.*

John Mackenzie, who had been Ken Loach's production assistant, became a director and started work on a play of mine about a bank robbery, *The Profile of a Gentleman.* George Sewell Junior was in the play as well as a young actor called John Bindon, a cockney from Fulham. He was a stranger to me and I cast him while I was listening to him talking in the bar at the B.B.C. He was unaware that I was standing beside him deciding whether he should be in the play or not. I nodded to John Mackenzie, put my thumb up and walked away. Both he and George Sewell Junior knew my characters like the back of their hands. They were the type of actors I needed. Unfortunately, rehearsals got a little bit held up. John Bindon, subsequently awarded the Queen's Medal for Bravery, given for his attempt to save a drowning man on a freezing November night, was held by the police while they asked him if he knew a murdered Chelsea model girl or any of her friends. A wealthy American was later convicted for this.

Another actor in the cast was pulled in for an identification parade by police investigating the Chelsea 'have a go' bank raid killing, after someone with a grudge had told the police he looked like the killer. After missing two days' work on the play he was cleared. I had a professional safeblower in the studio advising and he supplied me with a book which was not supposed to fall into the hands of undesirable people. It was published by the Safemakers Association. He was also in the play. Unfortunately, he made more money from being a burglar than from acting. He didn't last long.

During rehearsals George Sewell Senior telephoned me and I arranged to meet him at the Wig and Pen Club. John Bindon came with me. George Sewell Senior arrived and said if I gave him a thousand pounds he would say anything I wanted him to say. I told him that I only wanted him to repeat to the solicitor, David Napley, the story he had told my wife and I.

"I can do better than that," he said and produced a written statement from his pocket. I started to read it and was quite amazed. It was a complete confession to perjury.

> I first met Jimmy O'Connor just after Dunkirk, he seemed a very likeable chap and I very soon found out he was a money getter, I became manager of a night club and made him a member, he used to come to the club quite often and always seemed to have plenty of money. Well one night he came to the club and pulled me aside and said George how much would you want to have a club of your own. I passed it off as a joke and he then pulled me into the cloakroom and showed me about 7 or 8 hundred quid and then showed me a handkerchief with 40 or 50 rings, I said to him give me one of those for my wife, he said I'll be at your place to-morrow morning and she can have her pick. I then said I know how much you'll come, he then said, George, if I don't come take this watch and chain and keep it, well Jim did not come so of course I kept the watch and chain. Sometime after I borrowed some money from the Governor of the club (Izzy Farrar) and said to him take this watch and chain as a security. Well it must have been a good while after when Jim came to my place one Sunday morning and had breakfast, with my wife and myself and asked me if I could find him a garage for two lorries, well anyway while I was getting washed and dressed he went upstairs with my two boys, we went out and had a few drinks during the dinner hour and I left him; if I remember right he got some time. Well one Saturday morning my boy came into the passage and said Dad there is a man from the Yard would like to see you. I went into the kitchen and my wife then told me that a detective wanted me in the shop. I went out and he said good morning George, the Governor would like to speak to you. I said who is the Governor, he said Chief Inspector Nat Thorp, I said what does he want me for, he then said get yourself washed and

dressed and he will tell you when we get to the Yard, a squad car was waiting round the corner and I was taken to the Yard. I was taken into a room which was full of Law. I saw a detective whom I new very well, his name Jim Wakeling, I said to him what's it all about Jim? He said the Governor will be in here soon and he'll tell you all about it. Well in walks Chief Inspector Nat Thorp and he said I suppose you are wondering what its all about. I said yes, he then said well you are wanted for fucking murder, I felt like dropping, he then said at the same time pulling a package from his pocket and tearing the top off, have you seen this before, showing me the watch and chain that Jimmy O'Connor had given me, I said yes, he then said where did you get it from, I hesitated because I came to the conclusion it had been stolen, he then said did you notice anything on the back of it I said yes 10 years guarantee, he then said no did you notice any blood on it, I said no. Well he said if I tell you that watch belonged to a man that was murdered and his daughter has identified it what would you say, I said what can I say, he then said have you ever been with a man when a murder has been committed I said no, well he kept asking me different questions and nodding his head one way or the other meaning yes or no, at the time I was a crooked fellow and I might tell you I was very frightened, after a time I was taken into another room with me and Thorp on our own I said to him surely I have not been wearing a watch and chain that belonged to a man that has been murdered, he said no but that one will do, at the time I'm talking about a man I knew was doing some time at Pentonville and on that day I had a pass to visit him after being at the Yard a few hours I said to Thorp will I be able to visit this chap at Pentonville he then said I'll get you there on time, he ordered a car and I was taken home to get the pass and then on to the Ville but before I left Thorp told me that he would come to my place on Monday and see my wife, which he did, after that he came two or three times on his own. I got to know him quite well as a matter of fact I got permission to run a Gambling for six weeks I used to phone him each day and he would give me the O.K but I met him once a week to give him the necessary. After Jimmy O'Connor was sentenced to death I met Thorp and said to him what a shocking thing and he said they won't top him George don't you worry, on a different occasion he said to me I have got him eating out of my hand, at the time I got a very bad name amongst the underworld for giving evidence for the prosecution. I tried to explain to them how I was taken to the Yard and was under threats, well for years and years it worried me and at last I am glad to be able to tell someone all about it.

G. SEWELL

He had an appointment with David Napley that afternoon but refused to keep it unless I gave him money. I pointed out that it would make the statement valueless if I paid him for it, but said that I had advertised a reward in the *News of the World* in 1962 and he might be able to make a claim on it. George Sewell said he would go to Chancery Lane to see David Napley but was not going to give him the written statement. He left.

I telephoned David Napley immediately and told him that George Sewell was on his way and asked him to make a note of the fact that he had asked me for a thousand pounds.

After George Sewell left I asked John Bindon if he had overheard the conversation.

"If he'd been younger I would have hit him," he said. An hour later I telephoned David Napley and was surprised to learn that George Sewell had given him his own handwritten statement and had made another appointment to see him on October 18th. However, George Sewell was fifteen minutes early for that appointment at which he was going to make a full statement. He asked the secretary if he could re-read his previous statement to check a few points. Being a bit naïve, she gave it to him. As soon as he got it he stuffed it into his pocket and went down the stairs. Later he said he had nothing to say.

On January 1st, 1969, after two years of preparation, David Napley, my solicitor, submitted a petition to the Secretary of State. As a result the Home Secretary ordered an enquiry into my case. I was very pleased and felt there was some hope that I would be granted a free pardon, and proved innocent.

Later that month Nicholas Tomalin wrote an article in the *Sunday Times.* Ten days earlier he had been to see Ernest Thomas, who repeated on tape what he had already told me. Nicholas Tomalin asked him why he had not told anyone before.

"Well, he only got life, he ain't topped," said Thomas.

Nicholas Tomalin also went to see Mr A, who completely denied the charge. Later he and his brother went to see Ernest Thomas and persuaded him to withdraw his statement, but it still exists in my petition to the Home Office as well as on the Tomalin recording.

Finally, in November 1970, the Home Office agreed a statement with my solicitor saying that they had made a full investigation into my case and that certain features of the prosecution and the trial might be considered unsatisfactory. But they said that they could not reopen the case "on the basis of evidence and arguments already considered by the courts and will consider intervening only if there is significant fresh evidence which establishes beyond reasonable doubt the innocence of the convicted person".

As for the Home Office investigation, which concluded with Commander Wally Virgo in charge of it, George Sewell Senior retracted the allegation that he had been forced by the police to implicate me. Ernest Thomas, who also made a statement, declined to make another one and would not confirm or deny his earlier statement. Neither Mr A nor his brother were interviewed. The officer in charge of the investigation who was trying to find another witness told me he had failed to trace her.

At the time of the publication of this book, ex-Commander Wally Virgo (he retired two years ago) was on bail facing serious charges arising from his conduct in the C.I.D.

Surely the fact that it was established in 1942 that the watch was stolen from Bath completely destroyed George Sewell's evidence anyway. Why did they keep me in prison until 1952?

I suppose the answer to that is exactly the same as why they kept Oscar Slater in jail for nineteen years before he was granted a free pardon. Timothy Evans got his free pardon after they hanged him. I must have been a fool to have wasted my time trying to prove I am innocent, but I got half a loaf. There is an old cockney saying, "Half a loaf is better than none". Nevertheless, I am still labelled a murderer.

A few months ago I went to the Old Bailey. I wanted to listen to a trial. I asked to see Leslie Boyd, the Clerk, to get a ticket for the court. At the door a policeman refused me admittance to the administrative offices of the Central Criminal Court.

"It's a matter of identification," he said. Then he said, "I know who you are. I also know your wife. You can't come in."

"Well, if you know who I am why do I need some identification?" I asked. "And if you know who I am, what am I in your book? A writer, or a convicted murderer? Is that why I can't come in? Anyway," I said, "I'm going to do something you can't do. I'm going to the pub." I left the building and went to the Magpie and Stump.

After fifteen years of marriage Nemone divorced me. I find it very difficult to write about her. Many people have asked me to write about her. One writer ghosted a series of newspaper articles about Nemone and myself which were to be published under my name. Before signing the contract I read them. "My ears tingled when she came into the room," he had written.

"I don't want to upset Jack, the ghost writer," I said. "But I can't sign my name to this bollocks. I'll write it myself and he can have the money."

I talked to Nemone recently about writing this book and told her that the publisher wanted me to add some more to what I had already written about her.

"You can say I had green horns and smelt if it'll get you some money," she said.

Nemone is the mother of my two beautiful sons, Ragnar and Milo O'Connor. She is a good mother. She is also a writer. It has been suggested by many people that she wrote my plays, but she was only eight years old when I wrote my first play. In her last play, *Baby Blues*, I was portrayed as a drunken husband. As a result of this and all the injunctions and publicity over Nemone's divorcing me, I have certainly had a belting from the press these last few years.

Despite her counsel's statement during the divorce that she was "terrified of this man" and a recent story in the *Sunday Express*, a Beaverbrook newspaper, which implied that I was a bad parent and did not support my wife and two sons, we all four spent two months' holiday together on the island of Mykonos last summer and I do support them, as my bank statements show.

Mind you, I was no blue-eyed boy during our marriage, but that divorce destroyed both Nemone and myself financially.

I read recently in the *Sunday Times* that Theodore Goddards, her solicitors, had served her with a writ for £4,750. She has already given them £2½ thousand of our money for divorce costs. Another writ server came round with one for me for £1,500. That is nearly nine thousand pounds. Five years after she took out the first divorce petition and £40,000 shorter of hard-earned money, we are both broke.

I was walking down the Portobello Market the other day when a gleaming Rolls-Royce shot past me. The driver reversed back—it was Ted and Charlie who were at my wedding, now two tycoons living in the Surrey belt. Two great ex-sufferers, they got out of the back streets—both made it the hard way. Now, this was our first meeting for ten years.

We laughed, this called for a drink. I took them into a pub—my local. We had not yet spoken, just laughed.

"Well, how are you, my son?" said Ted. I nodded and smiled. I knew Charlie was weighing up the quality of my clothes. "Doesn't worry you, Ginger, having led the life you've lived to find yourself going the full circle, back at Portobello Road after the life you've lived, with Belgravia and the Jet Set? We were a bit worried about you—thought you might return to villainy again."

"Don't worry about me. I won't have to thieve again. You can never starve living among barrow boys and villains. Anyway, God gave me a gift." I pulled out my pen and pointed it at them. "*You're all* my material."

They drank up. I asked them to drop me at the Social Security Office in Bayswater.

"Oh, no," said Ted, "don't tell me you've come down to that!"

"No, mate," said I. "I am writing a play about those who draw it—*A Way of Life*—for the B.B.C. Papillon once asked me what I thought of life. I told him—life was one big joke, if you spend yours chasing money."

I felt good at being dropped at the door of the Social Security Office in a £20,000 Roller.